"Jason is an inspirational visionary and proven thought leader in the ever-evolving world of defining the future of work and the impact to the enterprise—this book is a must-read if you want to be on the cutting edge of workplace strategies for years to come."
—Chris Barbin, CEO & Co-Founder, Appirio

"Jason is one of the most thoughtful, foresighted people in the talent space today. This book distills his insights and ideas about where we are headed and how it will impact you. Read it!"
—Daniel Debow, Senior Vice President, Salesforce.com

"I have trusted Jason for advice and guidance for over ten years—as a client, a business partner, and a valued industry colleague. This new book provides readers with great insight on future workforce trends from someone who has always been at the forefront of our industry. I consider it a must-read for HR executives, practitioners, and service providers."
—Brian J. Kelly, Partner, Workforce Analytics & Planning Global Practice Leader, Mercer

"HR is constantly being faced with the choice to adapt or die, and Jason's book is a guide to staying relevant. Jason paints a holistic picture of how technology is going to change the way we think about HR—a must-read for yourself, your team, and your entire C-suite!"
—Michael Peterman, Director of HR Administration, Four Seasons Hotels and Resorts

"Jason is like no other. His brilliant and honest insight makes any business professional excited to make changes ASAP."
—Sally-Ann Cooke, Project Manager, The Consultant's Right Hand

HR FROM NOW TO NEXT

REIMAGINING THE WORKPLACE OF TOMORROW

JASON AVERBOOK

For more information contact:
info@jasonaverbook.com
Jason Averbook

ISBN print: 978-1-939758-36-1
ISBN eBook: 978-1-939758-37-8

Library of Congress Control Number: 2014904762

Printed in the United States of America

Why QR Codes?

You'll notice that there are QR codes throughout *HR From Now to Next: Reimagining the Workplace of Tomorrow*. In addition to showcasing some of the important (and interactive) technology available to us in the workplace today, these QR codes will allow you, as a reader, to access relevant content and videos to supplement what you're learning. It will also allow me to continue to update the text, so that it's more of a living, breathing document—something that can change with these exciting times. As you read along, scan the QR codes using a QR code reader to further unlock the world of tomorrow.

—Jason Averbook

I dedicate this book to my wife, Heather,

and my sons, Ben and Alex,

who let me pursue my sometimes audacious

goals and dreams on a daily basis,

as well as all of the customers,

partners, and overall HR and IT community

members that join me on this journey to

change the world on a daily basis.

I'm truly blessed.

CONTENTS

Acknowledgments

MUCH of this book has been about breaking down boundaries and stereotypes. Apart from the meat of the thing, which is to say reworking our view of work, one of the biggest myths that writing this book dispelled for me is the myth of the writer as lone wolf. Just as the new and future workplace is a world of collaboration and crowdsourcing, writing this book has been a team effort of countless colleagues, friends, and supporters, all of whom helped in their own way to bring the work to life.

As always, my family must top any list of people who deserve to be thanked and thanked again: My wife, Heather, for her unconditional love, encouragement, and support, and our children, Ben (9) and Alex (6), for their ability to help me see things through their eyes, for allowing me to share their amazing dreams for the future, and letting me play with them as the goofy adult that I am. I also have to thank my family for their support during the countless days and weeks I spend on the road as I pursue my dreams to transform an industry—thank you. I want to thank my mother, Marcia, and late father, Marshall, for always being there—whether in person or in spirit—and my sister, Shelley, for her constant encouragement.

My work family is just as important to me as my home base. I want to thank Heidi Spirgi, my second sister and partner at Knowledge Infusion, as well as Appirio and its leadership team, for their encouragement. I am also lucky to receive constant support and inspiration from industry leaders and friends. I'd like to thank Bill Kutik (who has been like a father figure to me), Row Henson, and other colleagues and friends who are moving the HR industry forward. It's been a thrill to join you on the ride. Naomi Bloom, Daniel Debow, and Paul Sparta deserve my unending gratitude for agreeing to read and endorse the book, as well as true leaders in the HR space—Dennis Berger from CDW and Michael Peterman from Four Seasons Hotels and Resorts. I feel so fortunate to have them kick off my book. Steve Farber, thank you for inspiring me to share my own story. Business professionals of the world, thank you for continuing to reimagine the workplace for tomorrow, and for making my work better with your drive and your ideas.

Finally, special thanks goes to Sally-Ann Cooke for driving me toward this end state. I approached Sally nearly a year ago with this crazy idea that I wanted to write a book, have it self-published, have it crowd funded, and get it done in a short period of time. Instead of saying, "No way, dude, not only have I never done this and I will never keep you focused long enough to write a word," she said, "Let's do it—I want to dream with you and make your dream come true." The body of work you are about to read came from my mind and vision but truly would not have been executed without Sally's dedication and professionalism, and to that end, I hope that we will always be partners in crime.

To my writing team, Michael Levin, Jenn Salcido, Sara Stratton, Rita Valencia, and others: Thank you for your invaluable support, guidance and advice, assistance, and editing.

And everyone else, most importantly the HR, IT, and business community—there's way too many of you to mention, even in this world of infinite e-space, thank you for your years of support. Thank you for everything.

See you at work (today and into the future).

Another infusion of knowledge...

An Invitation from Naomi Bloom, Managing Partner, Bloom & Wallace

EVEN though its name suggests otherwise, the Human Resources department isn't always something to which employees, managers, and executives love to turn. There's an unfortunate misconception about HR, one that's the backdrop for the oft-skewered Toby Flenderson in NBC's *The Office*—that it's inefficient at best, and frustrating at worst.

Fortunately for all of us, master HR consultant and global thought leader around the future of work Jason Averbook aims to flip that script. With firsthand knowledge amassed over two decades of experience, Averbook demonstrates in his relatable, engaging prose how the HR function must reinvent itself to earn its *seat* at the table—and how HR leadership can own that damned table.

We're living in a time of unprecedented change, in both degree and speed. Advances in information technology, from smart machines and predictive analytics to mobile everything and true software as a service (SaaS), when implemented well, greatly reduce need for HRM administrators even as they increase demand for great HRM strategic thinkers, policy/practice/plan designers, and data analysts. These technologies, along with robotics are changing the face, size, needs, and capabilities of the workforce, even as the most requested capabilities are in increasingly short supply. In short, there's a lot to keep up with—and Jason's book provides considerable help in doing just that.

HR From Now to Next is the roadmap for this change, centering around developing an outcomes-based strategic work and workforce plan, putting the right technologies together to make that plan operational, and ensuring that your workforce and HRM practices are THE source of sustainable business results. And this is a book that keeps on giving by using some of the same technologies to enable ongoing updates.

For forty-plus years, I've advocated (some would say scolded) business outcomes-based, technology-enabled HRM; this important new book takes that discussion to the next level. Jason Averbook is one of the leaders driving the HR world from now to next. Don't get left behind but rather join him on the journey.

Introduction

This Is OUR Opportunity

HR is a field that has the distinction of being one of the world's oldest, most necessary professions. From the beginning of commerce and organization of labor (and even before that, if we want to get down to brass tacks with our definition of HR), there have been men and women who have dedicated their careers to finding, managing, and maintaining talent. Those professionals operate behind the scenes, tending to any business's most important resource: Its workforce.

But being behind-the-scenes isn't good enough, particularly not now. The workplace is changing at mind-bending speeds, and the workforce is morphing along with it. New technologies, evolving leading practices, and an increasingly global, mobile working environment can yield amazing results for the corporations who can harness these developments successfully. And as managers of human capital, HR executives need to step out of the shadows and into the spotlight. This is our opportunity to not only revolutionize what we do within the larger umbrellas underneath which we operate, but to revolutionize what our companies can do, and what we can accomplish working together.

Looking Back on HR Over the Years

Like the operations manager who oversees the supply chain, HR executives oversee what I call *the people chain*. From the inception of the field, HR's primary responsibility has been related to managing risk and making sure people were paid and "somewhat" happy, how productive those people were, how productive those people could be, how to solve problems that were standing in the way of that productivity, and so on. But there is some hypocrisy inherent in this dynamic; in focusing on increasing the performance of its people, the HR function has spent more time measuring itself than the true performance of the workforce. Not in the standard ways—HR has always kept statistics on its turnaround for payroll, filling vacancies, and so on. But would an operations manager accept that the minimum markers were all that needed to be hit? Would a CEO tell his executives to stop pushing themselves, to stop discovering and utilizing new tools and technologies, to stop pressing for more possibilities?

Part of this pattern comes from the fact that while there are concrete and widely accepted metrics for measuring the performance of a product or the speed of a production line, there are not as easily accessible metrics for measuring the performance of a person. In the traditional sense, an employee could be measured by his output on the line; in the idea economy of today, it's not nearly so simple. So, in the past, HR has been unable to truly measure value in a way that shows ROI (Return on Investment). Absent of quantifying ROI on its "human capital," HR has been pigeonholed into another role—that of the prototypical paper-pusher, concerned only with tactical tasks.

Just because the obstacles may feel difficult to surmount, however, doesn't mean that this will always be the case. Focusing on mitigating risk, keeping the lights on, and pushing paperwork has earned HR the unfortunate reputation of the office policeman or the dull, rule-repeating bore (think Toby Flenderson on NBC's *The Office*—an unflattering character comparison if there ever was one). But now and in the future, if HR departments hope to stay relevant in their organizations and help push those businesses to be bigger, faster, and stronger, it's going to take a lot of hard work, a little elbow grease, and willingness to change.

I first noticed that higher-ups were ignorant of, and in some cases dismissive of, the capabilities of their HR teams twenty years ago when I was selling payroll services. For as long as they've been around, these payroll services have been early data warehouses for HR departments. Hypothetically, the databases included in these systems could help HR departments acquire and sort quite a useful array of information on their employees. However, it seemed to always be the case that these systems were only supplied with the minimum amount of data needed to keep the payroll program running.

The more I learned about the software I was selling, the more surprised I was by the lack of motivation and accountability for the HR department to make the most of its tools. Armed with this perspective, I began to notice that HR departments weren't being charged with the same expectations of achievement that other departments, such as production or operations, were held to. Things began to swirl into a self-fulfilling prophecy: HR departments weren't expected to do great things, so they did not expect themselves to do great things. Forget getting a seat at the table—what would they ever bring if they got there?

The good news is, as baffling as it may seem at times, that the changes afoot in the HR function are efficient, effective, and most certainly measurable. Gone are the days of vague proclamations and action items gone stagnant. This is our opportunity to move forward and get things done.

Why Change, Why Now?

Being in the space for over twenty years, I've worked with companies operating on all levels of this problematic (but promising!) turning point. I've had gold standard clients who really dove head-first into the HR revolution, seeing it as an opportunity to do better work for the company and have the company, in turn, do better work for its customers. I've had other clients who were still struggling with their department's role in the larger company and were looking to find some sense of belonging and balance before moving forward. And then, of course, there's everyone in between (or at least most people). But the key thing to think about is this idea of moving forward, because if you're not doing that, you're going to get left in the dust.

I see the impetus for riding the waves of this sea of change in the field as having a few parts. First, from a business standpoint, it doesn't make sense for HR to be operating in an adjunct capacity, pursuing little more than its own goals or implementing initiatives that aren't folded into the whole. Rather, good business sense dictates that the HR department needs to align itself directly with the C-level executives and the corporate missions of the organization, all of which are structured to grow profit, drive revenue, and increase customer satisfaction. When HR takes its expertise in human capital and applies that to the corporate objectives, this makes for not only a successful HR department, but also for a successful corporation.

It's quite apparent that CEOs are no longer content with listening to HR's anecdotal measurement of their own abilities where HR objectives are concerned. Rather, these C-level executives want to know what impact the HR department has from a *business* standpoint—the only standpoint that really matters to such executives. Their eyes, to put it bluntly, are not on HR's ball—they're on the company's ball, the overarching needs, and for the most part, many in HR just don't "get it" or know what to do about it.

This was certainly the case at a large insurance carrier where I was brought in to work on a major technology initiative. After implementing an applicant tracking system to make the insurance giant's hiring and review practices more efficient, the VP of HR and I went to the CEO's office to show him what we felt were positive results. The data point that we had in hand was that whereas it had taken this organization fifty-two days to fill a job in the recent past, it now took thirty-seven days; the technology that we had implemented had not only reduced the time to fill each position, but also provided us with an evidence-based metric to show ROI. The CEO should have been pleased, we thought; he was reducing expenses, customer waiting time, lag between employee turnover, and so on.

Needless to say, he wasn't as impressed as we hoped he'd be. His response was "It takes thirty-seven days to fill a job here? You have to be kidding!" In this case, I knew we were off base—we'd accomplished an objective that was absolutely in line with the overarching corporate needs, but something was getting lost in the translation. This CEO was essentially speaking a different language than what we were speaking in the realm of HR. While the metric we used to measure our efficiency—the speed of hiring—was enough to prove performance internally, we needed to present the data in such a way that it absolutely showed the corporate value of the project.

Not entirely back at square one, but certainly back at the drawing board, the HR leader and I looked to the data to see how we could better quantify the value of our contributions to the company's human capital. We saw that a fifteen-day decrease in the turnaround on insurance agents provided measurable financial gains for this company. On average, every insurance agent generated $750 per day for the company. When we carried that number out to the 3,500 agents that we'd hired since the project's inception, we were able to prove that our HR initiatives had generated a substantial amount of revenue for the company. When put to the CEO that way, he was hard-pressed not to see the value in our performance, with the ultimate takeaway from the situation being that HR needs to change not only the way that it measures its own performance in relation to the company as a whole, but the way that it presents that performance to the executives.

From the standpoint of talent management—attracting and servicing those employees who make up the most talented, effective members of the labor pool—HR finds itself at another crossroads. Whereas in the past, HR has concerned itself with being reactive to employee concerns in the best of scenarios (and being located under a mountain of protocol and paperwork in the worst), the present and future landscapes of HR are looking quite different. Just as the needs of the consumers have changed, driving the changes in corporate missions and motives, we can see a change in the needs of the employees serving these populations as well.

These employees, particularly employees culled from the Millennial generation, are eager for accessible solutions that inhabit flexible realms. Their fluency with immediate, responsive technologies makes them significantly less likely to be patient with methods that feel stale. These employees want to work with things quickly, each on his or her terms, and at his or her own pace, which is often faster than the typical call-and-wait model that HR has relied upon in the past.

These technological advances, when combined with a generational revolution and a reimagined consumer landscape, have created a perfect storm in HR. Enhanced data collection and analysis tools, more efficient streams of information and project management, and a more nimble, flexible workforce are all available to the HR department willing to see the potential inherent in such advances. And since the tools are available, all that leaves for us to accomplish is a philosophical shift. And while change isn't always easy, it is usually great.

The Eight Domains

During the two decades I've spent working with a diverse array of clients, I've identified eight domains that the HR and talent management spheres seem to revolve around. By reading this book and navigating through the eight domains of opportunity (and challenges) that now exist in the HR space, you'll be well positioned to take advantage of that change, whether you're working in the department, alongside it, or above it.

1. **The first domain should be readily apparent to you by now—of course, I'm speaking of technology.** We are living in an unprecedented time, a time when our toolkits are expanding rapidly and in ways that could scarcely have been imagined only years before. Because HR deals primarily in people, although not always face-to-face anymore, it's too easy for HR executives to write off the importance of their involvement in these technologies. But when you refuse to participate in this particular

revolution, you're not just branding yourself as a Luddite; you're leaving opportunity on the table.

2. **Next, we'll discuss how to create agility**, both in your HR department and for the business as a whole. As change is happening faster than ever, it's paramount that HR departments continue to evolve to keep up with changes in business models. As the talent manager, HR bears considerable responsibility for making sure that its company can continue to employ and empower a workforce meant to move the business forward.

3. **Finding the right people** is a vital part of this challenge. All the money, all the technology, and all the tools in the world won't be able to help you if you're throwing them in front of the wrong people. HR departments that truly understand their corporate directives and can translate those to methodologies that attract the very best candidates to accomplish those directives are HR departments that will not only gain a seat at the company table, but a well-deserved spot very close to the head of it.

4. Once the specific areas of need have been identified and the appropriate talent has been hired to fill those roles, the HR department must capitalize on the opportunities this talent presents by **focusing on—and continually increasing—engagement.** It's not enough to offer introductory paperwork sessions once this talent has been hooked. What can you, as an HR department, do to partner with the business and to create a more deeply engaged

workforce? Going beyond the administration of benefits and mitigating risks is not just advisable, it is absolutely necessary. By engaging your talent pool, you create a group of employees who enjoy what they do, look forward to going to work, and operate in alignment with the organization's goals. Greater engagement ultimately leads to greater retention as well, which means that the talent that you've put so much work into acquiring will be around to help push the company into the future.

5. In large part, **keeping your workforce engaged will depend on your understanding of how today's water-cooler works.** With more and more offices becoming decentralized hubs where major meetings take place rather than the center of a 9-to-5 universe, HR departments and the executives with whom they work need to adjust their methods when it comes to helping foster collaboration between employees. Looping again to the technology available at the moment and in the near future, there has never been a better time to look for new and exciting ways for your HR department to facilitate this collaboration. You shouldn't see these spaces as extras or nice-to-haves, either—there's nothing optional about incubating ideas for, from, and with your talent pool.

6. **Measuring the value of people** will always be a fundamental concern for HR. In this case, the lesson is that HR needs to look at the mandate it has always had—to be the facilitator for the company's human capital—and see how that capital can truly be measured in quantifiable

ways that easily translate to the other execs in the board-room. It's no longer enough to say that your human capital is invaluable; you must be able to assign a value. The fact that we know more about our laptops than the people who sit at them is quite indicative of why the "old" methods of thinking and measuring HR's impact are no longer good enough. We have an opportunity to harness data in entirely new—and ultimately more useful—ways.

7. Next, to truly push on and get the results that today's customers and companies demand, HR needs to **learn how to operate in an anytime/anyplace world.** Like the watercooler itself, the boundaries of the workplace have changed alongside the boundaries of the economy. Employees need to be able to deploy the tools, technology, and applications that they use in their jobs from multiple points of entry. Today's workforce relies on flexible time and space as well as tablets, smartphones, and the ubiquitous cloud. Companies that wish to stay alive—and to thrive—need to jump forward to understand that these implements aren't extras or optional niceties. Rather, they make *good business sense*—they are scalable and convenient and can be used to increase profit margins alongside employee efficiency.

8. Finally, **the HR department needs to take ownership of these technologies rather than foisting them upon the IT department.** While it may be appropriate for the IT department to configure the networks upon which these

technologies run, it's not good enough anymore for HR to simply wash its hands of the decision making when it comes to purchasing and deploying these tools. Understanding what the workforce needs is something that falls under HR's purview, not IT's—and in this case, the technology is merely a tool to augment the human capital. Throwing up your hands and stepping out of the fray cannot be an option.

••••

It may sound overwhelming; it may sound out of your comfort zone. I think that these aren't feelings to be afraid of. On the contrary, these are good things. As chief business innovation officer of Appirio, as well as over the course of my twenty years working in HR and technology industries, I can tell you from personal experience that the only way to change and grow is to push and to think differently. Some things may work, and others may not, but one thing is for sure—you can't be static. You must move outside of the realm of what's always been done and into the realm of what has yet to be imagined.

I'm happy to join you on that journey.

Chapter One

This Isn't Your Grandparents' HR: Reimagining the HR Function and Its Use of Technology

ALTHOUGH we must keep in mind HR's considerable history in the function of the workplace, we must remember that to look back and rest on our laurels isn't enough. If we're going to take advantage of the unprecedented opportunities that have opened themselves up to us at this moment, we must look around us for those tools that can help bridge a better way to the future. This pursuit of a better way for HR to play into the workplace isn't as lofty or difficult to grasp as you might think; through gaining an understanding of the larger economy and methodology of the world we live in today, HR leaders glean a clearer understanding of how to get from here to there—and sometimes even beyond.

Economies of Things vs. Ideas

On the highest level, the greatest indication that HR's future is long overdue for a major overhaul is the fact that, as a world, we've moved from economies of things to economies of ideas. Where manufacturing and all its subdisciplines were once on top, this has undeniably changed—in some ways for the betterment of all, and in some ways unfavorably for one interest group or another. The mill buildings that housed the industrial giants of the past have been converted into office space that incubates the next tech startups, biotech firms, cloud-based services, and other businesses of that ilk.

Whereas in the manufacturing economy of the past, HR and operations were able to count relatively concrete assets and liabilities—production numbers, manpower, machinery—in today's knowledge economy, people are the product as well as the means of production. HR is no longer tasked with counting machines, and instead now counts people. We must understand the value of those people, have a handle on who those people are and what roles they play, what skills they have, and how we leverage them in the best possible way. When HR execs tout people as a company's most important asset, it's more than just lip service—it's absolutely the truth.

Or it should be, anyway. The history of HR's modus operandi, particularly in some of the larger companies that have been around for a hundred years or more, unfortunately might indicate otherwise. These HR departments are set in their ways: Recruiting people the same way, hiring people the same way, and processing them the same way to get them started. Once the employees have been brought into the workplace through these channels, they then continue to interact with HR in very stale ways. Training and performance measurement typically remain stagnant, and employees are essentially forced into a bell curve with little recognition for the individual employee's strengths and weaknesses. Because performance is then lumped into that bell curve, compensation procedures become equally stagnant: Cost of living increases and blanket merit increases are applied largely across the board each year.

These standard procedures may have worked in a manufacturing economy, where worth was not just more easily computed, but typically more evenly situated. A certain level of technician merited a pay rate of one level, while the technician occupying the level above earned a slightly higher rate. Today, understanding and rewarding worth isn't as simple. The varied skill sets that make up the fabric of the workforce in the knowledge economy make every aspect of those workers more fluid. In order to retain talent and stay competitive, not to mention thrive as a business, truly investing time in reimagining HR's function to fit this new generation of workers is not just advisable—it's paramount.

This is not a situation unique to HR, of course. The changes happening the world over extend to other industries, which have also had to decide to respond and evolve—or fade away. Retail and education, for instance, have moved from traditional bricks-and-mortar establishments to farther-reaching, more nimble models. Students can access educational tools, including live lectures and course materials, anytime and anywhere. Shoppers don't have to wait for the stores to open in the morning to grab what they need when Amazon and other online retailers are available as swiftly as one can move a mouse around. Blockbuster Video locations are shuttered and vacant, while Netflix delivers instantly. Life has become plug and play, point and click—and there's no going back. There are no exceptions to this rule of the new reality; certainly not for a vital space like HR.

Why Hasn't HR Changed?

Unlike other segments of industry, HR seems particularly resistant to change—not just from within, but from without as well. And while part of the onus for this stagnation falls on the shoulders of the other C-suite executives who mark and encourage the corporate movers and shakers, often leaving HR out of the mix, it's equally a function of HR's own identity crisis.

Historically, HR has been seen as a reactive support function rather than a proactive profit driver. Whereas sales, marketing, and the like can be seen as departments that clearly collect and offer a catalyst for revenue, HR is a line item—an expense. HR needs to be staffed with employees who are charged with mitigating risk and keeping the lights on—and these aren't trivial contributions, by any means. For instance, HR is typically tasked with administering important sexual harassment and compliance training, or helping employees and companies document accidents and injuries on-site that may later on be submitted for worker's comp claims or, worse, litigation. To say that the HR department offers support rather than revenue isn't to minimize the contributions that HR *does* make. Be that as it may, there are no quantifiable revenue streams that come from HR. That's the part of the equation that isn't going to change: The HR department isn't going to take on a radically different *role* in any corporation, but this doesn't mean that it can't take on a radically different *approach.*

> The HR department isn't going to take on a radically different role in any corporation, but this doesn't mean that it can't take on a radically different approach.

As it stands, there's a generation of HR leaders who have become mired in the way things have always been. In order to gain the forward momentum that the industry demands, HR leaders need to stop being content with simply counting heads—making sure things run smoothly and everyone gets paid on time—and start making heads count. The new school of HR leaders are already doing this, and they are the most successful in leading, not continuing to follow, industry trends. These leaders are responsive to Generations Y and Z, workers who are not motivated by the concerns of their forebears, but rather have other things on their mind. These are leaders who understand that HR needs to go beyond its transactional approach, and instead truly become a strategic lever in the organization.

Change is inevitable, both within an organization and without, particularly where a business model is concerned. Something that seems standard and irreplaceable can be rendered an anachronism in the blink of an eye; the C-level executives in charge of things like product development, manufacturing, advertising, and so on know this instinctively. They understand that to keep their business surviving and thriving, and to truly keep the lights on, they might need to shift their strategy, their goals, and their methods at a moment's notice. When HR is aligned with the larger corporate goals, it can then move beyond the basic transaction—acquiring its human capital—and engage it, instead, in a more holistic approach that looks specifically to assess and fill the needs of the changing organization.

One of the clients I've been fortunate to spend time with is one of the oldest manufacturing firms in the world, which we'll call Company C. This company manufactures a line of traditional assets used in everything from home building to computing. A fine example of manufacturing, Company C's HR department has typically been most involved with managing unions, running as a go-between for their higher-ups to keep the relationship with the unions strong, functional, and working to the best of their ability. Because the unions supplied the human capital that Company C most needed—the people for its line jobs—having HR spend all of its time in this relationship made sense.

But as the world changed, and Company C needed to acquire some lateral interests and opportunities to stay relevant, HR found that the relationship with the unions wasn't necessarily center stage anymore. Instead, HR now had to manage teams of skilled engineers while the company moved from widgets to world-changing innovations. While working with Company C and emphasizing not only the value of change but the necessity that HR involve itself in that change, we were able to more fully align HR with the overarching organizational goals and the changing culture. And instead of falling flat, they're flying high.

Thinking Differently

In a world of changing product lines, changing industries, and changing expectations, thinking differently becomes much more than a catchy slogan; it's a necessity. Luckily for us, today's world is also home to that "perfect storm" for a paradigm shift in HR: Not only do we have evidence of the need for such a shift—we have the tools and technology to make it happen.

If we think differently about HR and look at it from without as opposed to within, avoiding that tempting, inward-reflecting performance mirror that's been used in the past, we can start to see the areas in which we need to continue to think differently. If we see that the organization needs to acquire and retain people with certain skill sets who tend to fall into these later generations, then we can change our goals and techniques accordingly.

The image on the next page is very simple, and this should be heartening for you, because the concept it espouses is equally so. And while accomplishing alignment will be a challenge for many, understanding the elegant simplicity of this foundation will go a long way toward illuminating some of these dark corners of questions: Where do I go from here? How will I get there?

As the chart shows us, one piece of knowledge informs the next step. If the corporate objectives are understood, the HR department can then develop its HR objectives. Once those objectives are clearly outlined, the HR technology objectives can be put in place based on that. But if one piece of the puzzle is taken away, then we're attempting to go forward without a map. This leaves us moving in circles at worst, and standing completely still at best.

The reinvention of recruitment and hiring practices gives us an excellent example of this alignment in action. Let's say, for example, that one HR department saw its organization moving away from a simpler iteration of itself toward a future that relied on employees who were savvier and better versed in strategy. Finding those kinds of employees is not as simple as posting on your website or job board ads that you're seeking strategic, skilled employees. To find these diamonds, it's likely you'll have to engage in active recruiting rather than passive recruiting, looking instead to headhunt them away from the competition. At that point, your company's HR team now knows the corporate objectives and the HR objectives, and can proceed to put better technology in place to make the objectives less of a wishful thought and more of a reality.

In large part, even when the technology used within a company changes (thanks to the IT department upgrading the systems, usually), the processes that the HR department employs with those technologies stay the same. This is a mistake that compounds with each of the inevitable iterations of software. If an organization has

Jason Averbook 2014©

moved from DOS to Windows 95 to client/server and so on, but the HR department is still using old methodologies developed with those older technologies, valuable opportunities for change and reinvention are left on the table. The people in the C-suite aren't the only ones who will notice this and feel distinctly underwhelmed, either; all of those Gen Y and Z employees that have been so hard to capture will sense that they might find a better fit elsewhere.

To avoid losing more ground each time an upgrade hits, we must again return to the alignment of corporate objectives, HR objectives, and HR technology objectives. One simple example of this is moving the process of performance reviews from a static paper document pulled out once a year during uncomfortable one-on-ones and moving these reviews (and resulting training) into real-time. Generations Y and Z are used to immediate feedback: If they post a family picture and get twenty "likes" on Facebook, they know their friends are engaged and supportive of them. If they see a link for an event and want to click on it, they can, and instantly have access to not only information about that event but ways to buy tickets, transportation options to get to the event, and a button to invite others to share in the experience. And these methods are already out there, humming along all over the globe.

In a faster moving, more globally connected workforce, HR can no longer afford to stick its head in the sand and ride the coattails of IT and its upgrades. They need to start steering, and the only way to go is forward.

Takeaways: This Isn't Your Grandparents' HR

1. **There is a place for HR in the organizational structure.** That won't change. The roles that the HR function needs to fulfill will still need to be fulfilled. By reenvisioning the HR space in a shifting world with changing technologies, I don't mean taking on a radically different role. I mean taking on a radically different approach.

2. **To be successful, HR leaders need to lead.** This means they should not follow industry trends. They have to be ahead of the curve and responsive to their changing workforce, particularly Gen Y and Z workers, who have different concerns and motivations than those that predate them around the office.

3. **HR needs to look out, not in.** For years, those in the HR function have looked inward to measure their performance. They stacked up their output against benchmarks that applied only to HR. This is no longer good enough. To achieve total and true alignment with the larger organizational goals, HR leaders should look outward instead of just inward.

4. **Write the map—all of it.** Once the HR department is able to look outward, it can truly understand corporate objectives and then set and align the HR and HR technology objectives. But if one piece of that puzzle falls away, we are attempting to move forward without a map. We'll get lost.

5. **If technology changes, processes must change.** One thing that often happens with implementing change is that a technology will be changed, but the processes that go along with that technology will be the same. This means that the same mistakes and inefficiencies will continue to be repeated. If we are to be the architects of true change, processes must change alongside technology.

Chapter Two

Change Happens Faster Than Ever: Creating Agility

BY now, you certainly know my party line on change. Change is good; change can even be great. But the most important thing for you to understand about change is that it's happening—with or without you. To stay relevant, to stay nimble, and to keep your seat at the C-suite table (or even the average conference room table, for that matter), you must embrace the change and try to stay in front of it.

This is not an easy task in today's world. Businesses are changing faster than ever, largely to keep up with external pressures from the consumers they serve and the marketplace as a whole. In the HR industry, the changes to contend with aren't solely external; rather, there's been a history of HR focusing on internal changes, almost to the exclusion of those important external factors. This is partially born of necessity—HR plays a vital role in the internal functions of the organization. But, as you now no doubt understand, for HR to continue to evolve and expand its utility as we move into the future of the workplace, these external factors cannot be ignored.

One of the primary forces driving this change is the increasing connectivity that exists in the world today. With the veritable g-forces of globalization hard at work, businesses around the world are no longer operating in isolation. Instead, they are much more built on strategic partnerships and alliances, sometimes breaking not only the boundaries of their state or country, but continental boundaries as well. Organizations now stretch across oceans, moving beyond the country where they were formed and into other countries where more specialized skills may be available, increasing efficiency in the process.

Change: People

Commerce and location aren't the only shifting pieces, either; the flow of information around and between businesses, their employees, and their customers has changed drastically, too. Now, instead of calling a complaint line or sending in a comment card, one can tweet a complaint and typically expect a response within the next one hundred tweets flashing across the feed. The Fortune 500 lists of the past few decades are littered with examples of companies that didn't respond fast enough to changing consumer feedback—**Blockbuster versus Netflix,** for example. In fact, of the companies on the Fortune 500 in 1987, roughly twenty-five years ago, only sixty-five of those 500 companies—just about 13 percent—remain active.

This in itself is a big change to witness; for some of the older generations, it's definitely caused whiplash. I remember my father working for an insurance company that *his* father worked for—for forty-eight years as compared to his father's fifty-four years. They were part of a world where companies lasted for a century or more. Now that we have these generations working side by side with the digital immigrants (like myself), people who grew up with pencil and paper and have to adapt to new technologies, as well as the digital natives—Generations Y and Z—the ballgame is radically different, even within the same organization or department.

Although I've been semi-successful as a digital immigrant, spending my career helping other digital immigrants understand how to gain and maintain forward momentum, I'm never at a loss for reminders of the disparity between these generations of workers (and workers of the future). One moment summed this up beautifully, I thought, as I attempted to take my then five-year-old son, Alex, for a haircut including a wash. This was a big step for him; for some reason, he'd never wanted the stylist to wash his hair after cutting it. After a long process of goading, coaxing, and bribing with candy, we went to the back room to the "showers," where Alex sat down in a chair. His head didn't reach back to the bowl, and the woman cutting his hair told him that she'd be right back—she needed to grab a phone book.

Alex, already suspicious and worried as it was, grabbed my arm, frantically asking: "Daddy, what's a phone book?!"

It was obviously hard to take his distress seriously, but apart from the humor implicit in the situation, I saw something larger at play. The phone book, a hard resource that I'd grown up using, was now relegated to something used to get one's hair washed. When we were leaving, he asked me why they even called it a phone book. I have to admit, I struggled to find an answer that was better than an endless loop that would mean nothing to him—his generation will never understand the need for a paper phone book when Google, at least for now, has a hard line right to their devices.

This story is also important because it's Alex's generation, and the generation of workers that have come just before him, that organizations and their HR departments are going to be working with as consumers and employees. These are horses of entirely different colors: They are motivated by different things; understand different things; think differently; live differently. Whereas my generation has a fundamental suspicion of some of the more "invasive" forms of technology available today (check-ins, our phone numbers being linked to our Facebook profiles, our photos being public property), the following generations don't have that allergy. They seek and give feedback freely; they, for the most part, don't separate their work and personal lives; and they expect a greater degree of transparency and agility in a workplace.

Change: Process

The second major area where companies need to be responsive to and initiators of change is in their *processes*. If the corporate landscape is changing, and the people within it are changing, it follows that the processes employed by these organizations must change as well.

Starting from square one, we can see how the HR processes, when left unchanged, can be frustrating and outdated, particularly for these Gen Y and Z workers who are used to a certain sense of integration and immediacy. The process of hiring a new employee or contractor and bringing them on board ("on-boarding") is a prime example. It's probably not a stretch to say that anyone reading this book can remember their first day at one of the companies they've worked for: Filling out stacks of paper, multiples of certain forms in some cases, to be sent out to different locations and departments for follow-up signatures and authorizations and so on. That process itself could take hours, but the interoffice mail deluge it triggers is no joke, either.

In today's world, the expectation is that a worker should only need to give his information to his company once: when he applies for the job that he eventually accepts. If an application (particularly a digital application) entails pertinent information, he feels that there's no good reason why the HR department that processes that application shouldn't retain that information for when he's eventually hired. And, I have to say, I agree with this typical Gen Y/Z worker. Why should he have to spend his valuable time, ostensibly time that now belongs to a company that values *him* and communicated that value by offering him a job, filling out paperwork about his full name in triplicate? In this case, HR is not treating this employee as their most important asset. If this employee were indeed their most important asset, they'd be remembering his name, just as you might remember the name of a business associate with whom you were attempting to create a lasting relationship.

From a business standpoint, this lack of efficiency makes little sense. And if HR is to truly align itself with the business acumen, it must understand that it needs to function in such a way as to support better productivity, not bigger piles of paper. Bringing an employee on board faster means less lag time, more engagement, quicker productivity, and therefore, quicker generation of profit. Culturally, while HR is a very important support function, there's a stereotyped expectation from within that HR "knows what it knows" and nothing else. While this was never ideal as an operational philosophy, it particularly doesn't work in an era where, for the first time ever, consumers often have access to better technology than the businesses do. The change in this technology is continual, and therefore the change in the processes that HR employs to work with these employees needs to be continual as well.

> For the first time ever, consumers often have access to better technology than the businesses do.

We're living in a time now that I call "perpetual beta"—where things are being tinkered with, tried out, and adjusted to. To thrive

> We can't sit on our hands and wait until the perfect thing is engineered, because by then, it will be long obsolete.

in a perpetual beta world, we need to be beta testers; we need to be beta *thinkers*. We can't sit on our hands and wait until the perfect thing is engineered, because by then, it will be long obsolete. The HR leaders that are successful today, and will continue to be successful tomorrow, understand this intuitively, using the tools at their disposal to collect data on their assets and their contributions to the business. This encompasses everything from analyzing hard figures on turnover, compensation, and proficiency to properly streamlining their warehousing of data when it comes to their employees. We can be much more agile and responsive when we don't have to ask an employee for their legal name ad nauseam.

Change: Technology

The third area aligned with the change in people and change in processes is change in technology. Fortunately for HR leaders, the change in technology that's underway now is not just a challenge to be met, but also offers a solution to some of these quandaries of how to keep up and keep going.

Ultimately, how to solve this problem isn't particularly easy—I don't mean to give you the impression that keeping open eyes and a more open mind is going to magically bring all of these factors into proper alignment. I think of the problem more as a Rubik's cube, where HR tries to balance and shift many moving pieces at once. This in itself is a somewhat overwhelming analogy, as not everyone feels particularly adept at conquering those colorful, complicated puzzles. But after years of helping companies unlock the Rubik's cube of their changing workforce, I can say with absolute certainty that one of the most basic, fundamental approaches that you can take to solve these slippery problems is to *focus*.

As I've said before, it's not enough to simply pay lip service to an idea—to write on your company website that you're dedicated to employing the latest technology in your field, or giving the impression on various social networking sites that you're a savvy workplace filled with savvy workers. It's certainly not enough to offload these technological functions to IT, asking another department whose responsibilities aren't in alignment with your own to help you manage *your* assets and resources. IT has their own issues to worry about, and they're good at worrying about them; HR should focus on its own issues, its own people, and its own assets. They know those assets best, so they have a fundamental insight into what those assets might need.

When properly focused on change and utilizing the technology that's become available, an HR department is aligned with the business philosophy of its higher level organizational goals. If the people in the HR department are dedicated to understanding the challenges and problems that are keeping them from changing or increasing productivity, then those same people can reverse engineer solutions, looking for technology to help bring those solutions to fruition.

In addition to yielding solutions, focus also brings a clearer sense of priorities for the HR leader with limited time and resources. By focusing on the things you want to be *great* at, you'll understand where your

> By focusing on the things you want to be *great* at, you'll understand where your time and energy needs to flow. What's left after this are the things at which you can afford to simply be *good*.

time and energy needs to flow. What's left after this are the things at which you can afford to simply be *good*.

Over and over again, many of the companies I work with will come to me seeking a silver bullet or magic wand that will help them reach greatness in the areas in which they strive to be great. They look to the gold standards in their industry, wanting to know what the secret sauce is for these standard-bearers. The bad news, I always tell them, is that it doesn't work that way. The *good* news is that you can still find a way to make it work, just by simply understanding that what makes an HR department good or great isn't a standard metric, but the concept of alignment with the larger organizational goals. Followers follow, and leaders lead by leapfrogging over the followers, finding their own greatness and exploiting their advantage.

Recently, I worked with a company that needed to overcome the challenge of catching their processes up with their purpose. While the company itself isn't particularly large—it employs about 3,500— its executives have a profit model that requires rapid acquisition of other businesses and the employees and assets of those businesses. This is what they've decided to be great at, and yet, something about their strategy wasn't working for them.

After a short time working with the HR executives in the company, I could see the problem quite clearly: Their aim was to operate as a serial acquirer of other companies and other technologies, but they actually had no processes in place to make this happen. Productivity was lagging as they were acquiring different assets with no way to fold those assets (and particularly the human assets that come along with them) into their larger corporate culture. There was a major disconnect between what they wanted to do (as well as how they saw themselves) versus what they were able to do. But the solution has

Jason Averbook 2014©

been in front of them the whole time—if they know their area of focus, they can then know what strategy to align themselves with.

The same goes for a food company I consulted for which had projected major growth spurts in market share in China and Latin

America, but had no ability to put systems in place to support their factories and sales teams in those countries. Their headquarters weren't flexible or mobile; they didn't have the employee base to communicate—literally, just to speak the appropriate language—with their assets in those other countries. The problem is simple enough to fix now that they've identified it, but it would have been simpler to be forward thinking and to put the appropriate translation teams in place to ensure a smooth entry into those burgeoning markets.

Beyond specific examples from my own career, I can see the implications across the field as they relate to the oncoming generational shift. The fact of the matter is that the clock is ticking: A large number of digital immigrants will retire, and the digital natives will take over. There's no point in denying the fact that this new generation will make up from 50 to 70 percent of the workforce over the next ten years; no matter how much we digital immigrants stick our heads into the sand, there's no escaping that we're getting older and we're going to phase out. To ensure proper positioning for the future of our industry and the industries we serve, HR needs to understand that changes in strategy and shifts in thinking are necessary. We must stay in front of change, training and staying agile and nimble like an athlete. It's going to continue to happen faster and faster, and if we count on other departments to help us or do the work for us, we can forget about sinking or swimming—we'll simply be lost under the thundering tide.

Takeaways: Change Happens Faster Than Ever

1. **Change with your workers.** The first major area where companies need to focus and to initiate change is with *people*. When new generations step into the workplace, for example, companies must understand the needs and desires of these new generations of workers. A company must develop a sense of its human capital, and how best to serve them so that they may serve the company's goals better.

2. **Change your processes.** Corporations are changing, too, morphing to keep up with the changing times. Technology and shifting marketplaces dictate these changes, just as generational differences have created alterations in the behavior and motivations of the workforce. If the places are changing, and the people are changing, the processes we employ in the workplace must also change.

3. **Be beta testers and beta thinkers.** There will never be a perfect time to launch the perfect product. In the shifting sands of today's marketplace—no matter which marketplace you're in—if you are waiting for the perfect time to launch something that's 100 percent done, your doors will close long before that will happen. Someone else will beat you to it. Successful HR leaders understand this on an innate level, and encourage thinking and creating in beta—a world of constant improvements and adjustments, rather than one big blowout launch.

4. **Technology is a tool.** One of the bonuses of all of this change, particularly in technology, is that it represents not only a mountain to be (gleefully!) scaled, but an opportunity for organizations as well. To keep up with the changes in the workplace and the workforce, organizations will need to embrace some of the new technology available—and this is a great thing. It can help smooth transitions, make companies more efficient, and ultimately add to the bottom line.

5. **Focus, focus, focus.** It's tempting to try to do everything all at once. Don't. First of all, you can't, and second of all, you shouldn't. If you take a strategic approach after understanding your overarching corporate goals, you'll be able to focus on what's doable, and moreover, what's important.

Chapter Three

How Does Your Bench Look?
Managing Talent

IN today's knowledge economy, talent is an asset that can't be understated. But it's not black-and-white—it's something that sits in the shades of gray. While laptops and real estate are concrete and predictable, talent is changing and flexible. HR leaders are largely saddled with the challenges associated with finding and managing this pool of talent, which has led to some pain points in even the most competent departments. However, in my view, challenges often present the perfect opportunities. With today's extraordinary talent pool—and the tools that these workers seem to understand and utilize intuitively—HR is presented with its time to shine. By working through what it means to effectively retain talent, develop talent, reward talent, and attract talent, we can then move forward into building a brighter, more innovative workforce.

What You Don't Know Can Hurt You

From a talent management standpoint, one of the most common problems that I see in organizations is that they struggle with knowing and understanding their talent. Often, organizations do not know what talent they already have, how to manage that talent, how to keep their talent, and/or how to be more forward in acquiring new talent.

Starting from the ground up, there is little quantifiable information that's understood and incorporated into the organization's practices in a strategic way. This may be because this is the way that it's always been done, or it may be because talent, as an asset, is harder to understand than some of the other more tangible company assets. Whatever the case, it's undoubtedly at the root of the problem.

Knowing precisely where the talent is situated is often an issue. Payroll is one thing—the HR department definitely has a handle on how much money they're shelling out and to which departments. But other than that, the understanding is murky. When it comes to the value of a laptop, they can say immediately, much like they can say about payroll, this laptop is worth $1,000. There's an asset number coded to that laptop, there's a certain amount of depreciation each year, there's a plan in place for when it becomes obsolete and where it will go next when a newer asset comes in. Likewise, most organizations know some basic information about each of their hires: They know their name, address, and department. All of this is easily accessed within the employee's personnel file. But anything further than that isn't necessarily a given—in fact, the information probably isn't there at all.

Generally organizations do not have a systematic handle on where their workers were hired from, how they heard about the position, what they want to be when they grow up, or what skills the worker has for the long term. All of these factors are important, particularly because they come heavily into play when thinking about how to get an employee to perform at optimal levels. Having this information on hand, and having a method and context with which to view it and understand it, is essential to building an agile and real-time talent management strategy.

Knowing that most organizations don't have a handle on this information, it shouldn't surprise you to hear that most organizations can't claim to have such a strategy. The less that's known about the specific employees within an organization, the less there is that can be known about the specific roles that those employees perform, and how those roles operate as part of the high-level, holistic view of the company. Let's take, for example, a car rental agency. If I'm at the top of this agency, I have a general idea of what I need: I need people to service the cars, I need people to order the cars and keep the inventory, and I need people to physically situate themselves at a desk where they can rent out the cars to customers. I need to have a call center to help with customer intake and reservations.

But if my car rental agency is like most companies, this is where my knowledge stops. They haven't put any value to those positions—They are not sure which positions are truly *pivotal* positions. In their mind, they're all the same, and in the mind of my HR department, all of these employees are processed and treated equally—the same information is collected (or not collected). But this is truly a fatal error. In reality, there are positions that are more important than others from a talent management standpoint. This is not to belittle any hardworking person's contribution to their company—this is only to state the plain and simple fact that there are positions that are harder to fill with the appropriate talent. These positions are more important to the overall success of a business, going beyond the purely necessary and moving toward the more long-term view. These positions require employees that are the hardest to acquire. If we can truly inventory and understand what talent we have, we can build a talent acquisition and management strategy that will help us move forward.

This isn't a revolutionary idea by any stretch of the imagination, but it happens to be revolutionary to a number of HR departments. However, there are examples that HR can look to for inspiration. One of the most accessible and, of late, better known examples of this is professional sports. With the Academy Award-nominated *Moneyball* having situated itself into the mind of the general public, whether they know it or not, many people have an idea of what statistics and data can do in the way of putting a talent management strategy in place and seeing demonstrable results from that strategy.

In the film, Jonah Hill's character uses data that everyone in his industry (Major League Baseball) has at their fingertips. This data isn't something that he's scouted personally, and it's not something that sits in a secret, gilded vault that only he and his team have access to. On the contrary, he's seen as little more than a bean counter in the scope of things, while the big, blustering talent scouts at the table scoff at the idea that he could possibly understand anything from hard facts and figures that they couldn't read from the swing of a bat or the spin of a fastball after decades of personal experience watching the best of the best (and the worst of the worst). But in binders and binders full of stats about each player, each game, each pitch, and each hit, he cracks the code.

He assigns values to the talents that the players possess, building a database of who bats well against right-handed pitchers or left-handers, who hits best on the outside and on the inside, who pitches better at night or during the day, and so on. So the first thing he's done right is to collect data on his talent, and the second thing, the biggest thing, *the best thing*, is that he put a system in place to engineer optimal performance from each person. He doesn't have a silver bullet—he's not using the billions of dollars at the disposal of some of the bigger teams to cast a wide net for the most talked about talent. He's precise, almost surgical, in his search for and understanding of his assets. And although many businesses don't yet have the capability that major sports associations do in this regard (their statistics are exhaustive and complete, by nature of their particular business), that doesn't mean that we can't strive for something appropriately scaled given our own resources and capabilities.

There's something more insidious than underperforming and leaving money on the table that can happen when it comes to not understanding or properly managing your talent. And I don't mean to be alarmist here, but if you're truly aligning yourself with the perspective of your C-suite, I think they'd agree that insidious is the perfect word for what might go on. Here, I speak of course of the competition spiriting or stealing away your assets. Not knowing what and who you

> If LinkedIn knows more about your assets than you do, your competition does as well.

have in your stable is a surefire way to lose them—and quickly. If LinkedIn knows more about your assets than you do, then that means the competition isn't far behind.

So what's a forward-thinking HR exec to do?

Recruiting

The first step in the process of talent acquisition, management, and incenting is obviously recruiting. When I say that this entire process is ripe for reimagining from the bottom up, recruiting is one of the foundational steps, and one that shouldn't escape editing and reshaping from HR.

In the past, the standard way of acquiring talent was to post a want ad. This morphed along with web capabilities, and companies began to post open positions on their websites, to industry Listservs, and then to third-party sites like Monster.com or Jobs.com. But like all things in today's supercharged world, the utility and audience for these sites has changed, particularly now that sites like LinkedIn and even the more casual-seeming Facebook have been able to cut out the middleman in recruiting and networking interactions. Now, these listings (including those on the company's own website) tend to attract what I call "drive-by" applications—where prospective employees fill out a generic application in an effort to get their name thrown in a large pot swimming with thousands of other applicants for any and every position. These applicants may be fine to fill some positions, but searching for someone for a highly skilled position in this kind of mess is even less likely than finding a needle in a haystack.

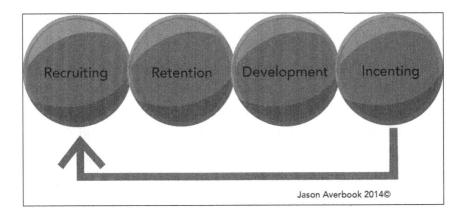

Jason Averbook 2014©

Now, successful companies have and must continue to move from this passive search to a more active model. These companies and their HR departments should actively source and procure different types of people to fit the specific needs that they've identified (again, going back to the *Moneyball* example of understanding what you have and then need before attempting to go and get it). How do I manage this? To give you a small example, we can return to that venerable thievery tool (I'm only kind of kidding, here)—LinkedIn.

So let's say that I know that what my company really needs today is a good writer. I visit LinkedIn, and search for business writers in my area from within my network (and sometimes even within the connections of those in my network—people who can be vouched for by trusted sources I already know). I might find a few good candidates, but I might find more than a few, in which case I could begin to build a talent community—a list of potential hires that I can start to court in one way or another. I could send them intriguing emails, call them on the phone, include them in my blog updates, and show them all the ways that it could be great to work for my company. I can tailor my messaging to their skills, and target with precision and efficiency. While I might not be outright head hunting, I'm certainly planting a seed in the minds of these potential hires. And when they're ready to start looking, my company will be top of mind.

This may sound simple—and it's definitely easier than you might think. But this doesn't mean that there isn't a great deal of planning involved. You'll notice that in each chapter of this book, we've discussed opportunities for change and for creating a solid forward momentum. Those opportunities are definitely there, and ready to be harnessed. But in order to really make the most of those opportunities, we need to think strategically, planning ahead for what we need. If we know what skills we have and what skills we need, we can use the new tools that are available to us to acquire the workers with those skills. But if we haven't put the time and thought into making an inventory of who we need and why, all the tools in the world are not going to help us very much. The same goes for headhunters, who are wonderful at doing a one-time job (at a hefty price to your company), but who won't be able to help you in a sustainable way in the long term, as much of your workforce retires over the next decade or so. Your company needs to own and be the best in the world at finding and bringing talent into your organization on a continuous basis, period.

Retention

Once talent has been identified and acquired, you must immediately move into understanding how to retain that talent. Retention can take many forms, and it can be as simple as tracking your human capital, seeing how long they stay and where and why they go when they leave, and it can be as complex as making sure your employees are always engaged, meeting goals and objectives, and understanding all the issues that can crop up around succession planning for when they leave.

Focusing on retention shows us one of the truly broken areas of HR. The very fact that recruitment and talent management has been portioned off into its own silo means that the head of recruitment doesn't act in alignment with the person in charge of retention and the person in charge of incentives. Or, if these are all the same person, that person is functioning in a separate and somehow self-contradictory world wherein they have to be concerned with finding new talent but are somehow tasked with retaining the current talent. This is a recipe for disaster. A recruiter has no time for an asset once that asset has been acquired—the very nature of their job is that they have to return to recruiting more talent, so the retention side of that person's job naturally falls by the wayside.

It seems relatively simple now that I've said it, but for me, it wasn't always so self-evident. It took a meeting with a brilliant but slightly contrarian CEO to bring the issue into focus for me. He had confided in me that he saw recruiting as "the dumbest function in business." As an HR consultant, I more than bristled at the idea, and so I challenged him. How could he say that, I asked, when recruitment was the very thing that enabled his company to do the work that it did? If it weren't for recruiting, from where would he get his workforce?

It turned out that his point was a little more nuanced than I was initially making it out to be. By saying recruiting was the "dumbest function," he wasn't talking about the act of actually recruiting talent, but the fact that recruiters keep their jobs by recruiting people, which is great for the recruiter. But if their jobs were truly in line with the best interests of the overall business, it would be better for everyone if recruiters started to think about keeping the people that they've just recruited. What he was advocating, and what I now see as an essential point for revision, is that recruiters should reframe their job as *talent managers* versus solely recruiters.

Once these leaders have reframed their positions, they can begin to dismantle the silos that previously separated all of these considerations that make up these complex human assets. They can use information available to them from things like performance reviews, understanding how well each employee contributes to the goals and objectives of the business as a whole rather than just their individual job. They can measure feedback they get from employees on benefits and continuing education in real-time, rather than sifting through vague feedback months later. And they can then be prescriptive about what the organization needs to do to get better. Improvement in all the aforementioned areas will no doubt help organizations stay relevant and competitive when it comes to retaining their talent, a consideration that is particularly important in today's fast-changing employment climate. Workers in Generation Y and Z move around more than any of their predecessors, seeking new experiences, new skills, and new types of appreciation beyond the traditional model of compensation.

According to *Unlocking Generational Codes*, an excellent resource by Anna Liotta that unpacks this phenomenon as it pertains to the workplace, Gen-Xers, the Millennials/Generation Y, and the "nexters" (or what I refer to as Generation Z) all have demonstrably different motivations and reactions to today's workplace.

In interviewing many of these X, Y, and Z workers throughout the text, Liotta uncovers some very candidly expressed sentiments about just how differently these generations view work in the context of their lives. She quotes a 2008 Aplin Recruiting survey of 3,000 workers entitled "Gen X and Gen Y: What Do They Want?", in which 96 percent of all Millennials surveyed said that the opportunity for growth was most important to them, as opposed to Gen X respondents, who ranked growth as a lower priority. To retain these workers, organizations will need to spend some time familiarizing themselves with—and aligning their goals with—their values.

Finally, the flipside of the retention issue is succession and succession management. In the past, this term has primarily applied to the C-suite—big executives whose departure would be sure to rattle an organization. But you'd be surprised to find out that today, particularly in the knowledge economy, the most important spokes in the wheel aren't necessarily the folks in the corner offices. According to one technology company I worked with, the most important jobs were that of the engineers who were developing the future product line. While a good executive isn't exactly easy to find, the types of compensation and benefit packages that are offered to that echelon are rather persuasive, and those folks are exceedingly able to take on new risks and relocate their families, rather than those at the bottom or the middle of the totem pole who are just getting started.

Succession is a vital consideration when ensuring the long-term health of your company and the happiness of your employees. If there is no plan for when the important assets in your company move on, then those that are left behind are going to feel uncertain of what to do, unsure about the future, and often unable to keep up with the stress heaped upon them in the interim. If there have been annual check-ins or real-time assessments of who the next in line for each position should be, this stress can be avoided.

Development

Part of planning for the long-term goals of the larger organization, and certainly part of executing proper succession planning, is developing existing employees. The development of internal assets to not only do their jobs better but also be able to transition to the jobs of the future, should certainly be a major aim for HR. And while many companies do already offer training of one kind or another, either internally or by reimbursing employees for classes taken outside of the organization, I've found that their approach is often lacking in that tactical precision that the best organizations employ so well.

One of my favorite, most cringe-worthy stories I use to illustrate this point comes from a large media company that had spent hundreds of millions of dollars on employee training, rolling out initiatives, and making sure its employees knew what was available to them. That, in and of itself, sounds great. But when I asked them what the top three training initiatives pertained to, their answer was lackluster: Word, Excel, and PowerPoint. When we asked the business what its employees, most of them very highly skilled engineers, needed to do their jobs, they answered: Knowledge of corporate values, foresight regarding the future of mechanical engineering, and customer service skills.

I don't think I need to point out to you that what they were working on didn't match up with what they really needed to know. If the HR department were to have properly aligned its training initiatives with the overarching goals of the business, all the time and money would have been better spent, and its employees would have been better prepared for the changes to come.

This kind of alignment can be achieved through transparent discussion through the corporate chain, but there are also more small-scale, real-time ways that this can happen. One is by actively soliciting and collecting real-time feedback from employees on the various learning events that they complete. If I have an employee who gets terrible feedback on her writing from a manager telling her that her writing needs work and she should take a class, that's not going to go much further than hurting her morale. But if the manager is able to put this information into a performance feedback tool and provide it to the employee along with a videotape (okay, not a videotape but a video clip) that is an educational snippet or webinar, and then can see that the employee has completed it, a different chain reaction is triggered. The manager identifies a weakness, the learning system fulfills a need, and the manager can track the outcomes—positive or negative. This offers real-time, strategic performance development opportunities rather than just throwing a bunch of spaghetti at the wall to see what sticks.

Incenting

The final area of consideration is one that's particularly tricky to navigate. Part of talent management is, of course, offering incentives to those talented assets that we hope to retain. Unfortunately, HR has been behind the curve on this as well—continuing to do what's comfortable and what has always been done and hoping that it continues to work for the workforce of now and the workforce of ten years from now. Each year, the department might conduct a performance appraisal, give a rating on each bullet point of that appraisal, and allocate a once-a-year pay increase based on merit.

I can tell you that this is problematic at best. For one thing, the workforce of tomorrow isn't interested in meager pay increases. Different things drive Generations Y and Z. They care about what kind of supervisor they have, or what kind of opportunities they're given to advance their career in the long term. They are prepared to make less out of the gate for a more satisfying job with greater prospects. They don't want to don a gray flannel suit and make a comfortable middle income; they're much more willing to risk accumulation of wealth now for greater riches (both monetary and intellectual) down

Jason Averbook 2014©

the line. Purely incenting based on merit increases is akin to offering a peanut butter spread of compensation—I'm spreading my knife over the entirety of the bread, telling all of my employees that I value (or don't value) them equally, when this is in fact not the case. We know that there are certain jobs that are more important than others, just as we know there are workers we're going to need to try harder to retain.

The new school of HR recognizes this and is responsive to it. A major retailer that I worked with did an excellent job of surveying their employees—particularly those on the upward swing who would be taking over when the workforce of today retires in a few years—and the results ran contrary to their expectations. They found that employees were much more apt to care about their feeling of involvement with others in their workplace. Those workers were looking for communities—the kayaking club or an LGBT association, for instance—rather than pay scales. These employees felt more connected to their community, more engaged, and more apt to stay and thrive rather than look elsewhere.

The lesson here, as with other points in the book, is that there's no one-size-fits-all incentive solution, just as there is no silver bullet for acquisition or retention. You must take a long, hard look at your organization and understand its goals, understand the goals of the people who make it up, and then try your hardest to offer something that fits with those goals. Then, and only then, will you attract the right kinds of people, make the right kinds of choices, and keep the right kind of momentum going.

Takeaways: How Does Your Bench Look?

1. **Know your employees.** More is always more, in the case of vital information about employees. The more you know about your employees, the better you can truly understand their role in the organization. From there, building an agile and real-time talent management strategy is possible.

2. **Plant the seeds to recruit rich crops.** You should always be developing new talent, getting that talent ripe for the picking. Tools like LinkedIn and other social outlets, including professional affinity groups, give you access to hundreds—if not thousands—of potential star employees. Look for ways to communicate your value to these potential hires and you'll be well positioned for when you've got a position to fill.

3. **Once you've got talent, you have to keep talent.** Retention isn't something that you "just get around to" when you think of it. It's something that must be considered in advance of obtaining talent so that you may immediately focus on retaining that talent.

4. **Don't overlook real-time feedback.** Real-time feedback, which is all the more possible with today's technologies, can help organizations stay nimble and aligned. Real-time means that changes can be made fast enough to matter. This is crucial for the development of existing

talent, particularly where performance feedback and training are concerned.

5. **Skip the peanut butter, pass the jelly.** Don't rely on a "peanut butter spread" solution such as merit increases across the board. Instead, do your homework on your workforce. Think about what they respond to, and what they would like to see. You must communicate that each person has a unique value to your organization—and moreover, truly believe that.

Chapter Four

How to Keep Your Talent: Increasing Engagement

IF you've put in the work to know and find the talent your organization needs, great. Fantastic, even! That's no small feat, particularly at a time when you have to proactively reach out to applicants (many who are not looking for a new position) as well as sift through the sheer number of resumes coming in—some from strong applicants and others, not so much. But unfortunately, now isn't the time to stop pushing forward. Now that you've amassed your appropriate talent pool, you owe it to them—and to your organization—to cast an eye toward keeping them engaged, for both now and for the long term.

When we're talking about engaging the workforce, we're talking about something that's been heavily researched and shown to be one of the true measures—and catalysts—for workforce success, productivity, and retention. Even if you're familiar with the essence of engagement, you might not be familiar with the term. We'll just define it up front, for our purposes, as employees being emotionally committed to their company and its goals.

Engagement is a hot-button issue in various sectors. Customer engagement is central to branding, and audience engagement is central to industries like advertising and entertainment. So no one should be a stranger to the idea of engagement, nor to the need to understand what the targets (in this case, the talent managed by the talent managers) are thinking and feeling. Be that as it may, most organizations still find themselves struggling with engagement. Industry estimates provided by Towers Watson per their Global Workforce Study show us that just over a third (35 percent) of their 32,000 survey respondents could be classified as "highly engaged." If that number sounds scary to you, it's because it is. Even the big guns are feeling the pressure: In an interview with *Harvard Business Review*, Doug Conant, former president and CEO of the Campbell Soup Company, references a terrifying internal statistic: When he first began his tenure at Campbell, he found that for every two employees that were actively engaged, one was not. That was certainly frightening enough for him to take seriously, and I don't blame him. Part of the reason it's so scary is because we simply don't know yet why that figure is so high—and getting to the bottom of the mystery is one of the Holy Grails for HR.

Considerations for Engagement:
Alignment and the Changing Workforce

In a beautiful turn of synchronicity, it so happens that all of the research done in this space shows that one of the biggest drivers for engagement is our old friend, alignment. Much as the HR function is at its best when aligned with the larger corporation's goals and objectives, the individual employee is most engaged when he is aligned with those same objectives. All of the benefits of feeling like he's part of a larger team with a greater purpose bolster his engagement, his commitment, and the overall quality of his work. A better workforce is self-perpetuating—employees will thrive in an environment where others are thriving and doing good work. Conversely, in an environment where it's clear that there's little direction or purpose, employees will continue to perpetuate those undesirable qualities. Knowing this, HR leaders need to consider how best to first align themselves with the overall goal and purpose of the organization, and then to impart that alignment to the workforce, staying vigilant to avoid being out of alignment.

Apart from alignment, the fact that the workforce itself is changing philosophically and demographically is another important consideration when looking at how to drive engagement. As the world has changed, and the generational composition of the workforce has changed along with it, so has what engages people. Whereas workers in my father and grandfather's generations were engaged by things like pension plans or job security, or the ability to truly clock out and come home at 5:00 p.m. with nothing more to worry about than how to relax and enjoy their evening, workers nowadays have different priorities. The more global composition of companies has also worked to uproot ideas of engagement from a static proposition to a more dynamic one. This dynamism seems to present a challenge not only from the standpoint of attempting to engage, but also from a measurement standpoint as well—which, since we should always be thinking strategically, goes hand in hand with implementing strategies for engagement.

How We Measure Engagement Now

The reality is that there's no one single metric that can give us a complete and accurate picture of engagement. Just as there's no silver bullet to *create* engagement, either. There are multiple angles: Retention, performance ratings, success in recruitment, etc. All of these angles are important, but going back to the notion of alignment—your organization needs to measure what's important to your organization, otherwise, you're looking at apples and oranges. If you have an idea of what's important to you (your goals and objectives), then you can measure engagement by that personalized metric, and then and only then can you implement strategies to drive that particular type of engagement.

In the past, and even still today, most organizations don't measure engagement strategically. They cast a wider net, doing rote engagement surveys of their employee pool once every year or so. The frequency is problematic in and of itself; think of a year in your own life. Have your priorities changed in that year? Have your circumstances changed in that year? What about two years? I'm willing to bet the answer is yes, and certainly, in that order.

Moving past the issue of how often these surveys are given, the very idea of the "anonymous" engagement survey given by the HR department is suspect to most employees. Those that take it seriously, and many won't, will probably feel threatened by the notion that their feedback will somehow come back to bite them. They self-censor, and the data are inaccurate from the beginning. After that, the data makes its way through different scrubbers—first, the managers, and then the HR department—who decide what to emphasize and what to downplay. By the time these survey results reach the executive ranks, they're outdated, drastically watered down, and far from an accurate picture of engagement. What happens then is that any initiatives taken by the organization are likely misguided or too little too late—they are not strategic, precise, or even in the ballpark.

Not having an accurate understanding of your workforce's engagement is exponentially problematic, like compound depreciation (rather than interest) on an investment. When you don't have a picture of engagement, it results in misaligned work—that is, employees who aren't working in line with the corporate goals and objectives, which are the same employees who are then just showing up for work without putting their passion, love, and energy into it. This leads to turnover, and pretty quickly. If an employee doesn't feel like he's engaged, he's at a much higher risk for leaving, particularly if he's part of Gen Y or Z—workers who are even less likely to be engaged if the work isn't meaningful to them.

More than a standard survey, measuring engagement ties directly into essential tasks and best practices for talent managers, because it ultimately determines what the talent management strategy needs to be. Again, we're back to gathering useful information and reacting appropriately rather than throwing all that spaghetti against the wall. While the former method can result in some positive changes, the latter method only ensures that things will get messy.

Food for Thought: Real Talk About Lack of Engagement

Lest you think this is a scare tactic I'm trying to pull out, I'll let the evidence from the ground level speak for itself. The leading polling firm Gallup put together an excellent report in 2013 entitled "State of the American Workplace: Employee Engagement Insights for U.S. Business Leaders," in which they reviewed over 25 million responses to an employee engagement survey over a period that stretched back to 2008. Some of the facts contained within might be eye-openers for you; some might be old hat. But I encourage you to think about them.

✓ "70 percent of American workers are not engaged or are actively disengaged."

✓ "Gallup estimates that these actively disengaged employees cost the U.S. between $450 billion and $550 billion each year in lost productivity."

✓ "They are more likely to steal from their companies, negatively influence their coworkers, miss workdays, and drive customers away."

✓ "Gallup researchers studied the differences in performance between engaged and actively disengaged business/work units and found that those scoring in the top half on employee engagement nearly doubled their odds of success compared with those in the bottom half. Those at the ninety-ninth percentile had four times the success rate of those at the first percentile."

Measuring Engagement in Real-Time

The first actionable item in this process is reimagining the problematic timeframe. Truly understanding engagement is a real-time need, rather than an inconsistent, intermittent survey every year or two. We need to listen to the buzz happening *today* rather than looking backward at a static survey. The dynamic culture of the new workforce (and the workplace itself) means that things are constantly in flux. If we're talking about a public company announcing its earnings, that has an impact on the workforce. If a member of the workforce suffers from a life-threatening illness, that will have an immediate impact on the workforce. If there's an accident at a workplace, that can cause a ripple effect.

The fact that the workplace is such a dynamic entity means that our measurement needs to be responsive to that; we need to step away

Jason Averbook 2014©

from static measurement tools and toward something that resembles a geothermic map or an election year polling graphic. If engagement is down in one division, we need to know about it when it happens. If engagement goes up, we need to know that, too. This specific, strategic, real-time measurement ensures that we're not spending our time on areas that may not need our help—or ignoring areas that desperately need our attention.

Forming an Action Plan

Once an organization has come to the understanding that the need to measure engagement is fast, fluid, and happens in real-time, it must then come up and continue with a plan to act on the information that was acquired. Here, HR can look to the proven strategies of some of those other industries—advertising, television, radio—and start to think of understanding and driving engagement in terms of audience analysis. If employees are the audience, it is important to understand what they care most about, what stokes their passions. This will allow HR to better drive engagement.

For every organization, and every workforce, these motivating factors will be different, as will the strategies. An organization could drive engagement by targeted, job-specific training—in my experience, the greater training an employee has, the more empowered that employee feels, and then the more engaged that employee is. An organization could drive engagement by communicating with people openly about company goals, and by involving employees in tasks like creating their own succession plan, giving them the sense that they have the potential to move up the ladder. A corporation can drive engagement by having its employees become active in the recruiting process, paying them for referrals. Like I've said before, there's no silver bullet: Understanding what's most important to your employees and to your organization should help drive your strategy.

That having been said, one constant, standard factor that I've seen positively impact engagement levels is communication and interactions. We'll talk about this later when we get to the culture of teamwork and collaboration in today's working world, but it bears mentioning now, certainly. If a company fosters open communication and interactions within its organization—not just between equivalent employees but also between subordinates and supervisors all the way up the chain to the CEO—employees will feel more engaged. If the workplace is seen as somewhere where everyone, including those at the top, is considered to be a facilitator, not a barrier to communication, the workforce will certainly feel more engaged. However, if the workplace is somewhere where an employee can walk in in the morning and make his way to his cube and sit there all day without speaking or interacting with anyone, he's not going to feel like he's part of a community. This isn't to say that solitary or flex-work situations are barriers to engagement and communication, either; though the tools and the geographic location may change, particularly in today's global environment, the fundamentals of good communication and community should stay the same.

Takeaways: How to Keep Your Talent

1. **Alignment drives engagement.** If your workforce is aligned with your organizational goals and objectives, they'll be engaged in the mission. The only way to get the troops engaged is to make sure the HR enterprise is itself aligned. This will result in the attraction, hiring, and facilitation of an engaged and aligned workforce.

2. **Measure what matters to you NOW.** Don't look for what's important to another organization in terms of engagement; see what matters to your organization and identify your goals and objectives around that. This personalization will give you an engagement metric that matters instead of more noise to sort through.

3. **Engagement should be a measure of NOW.** It's not enough to provide a survey every other year. It's not enough to provide a survey every year. Constantly measure the buzz—put your ear to the ground, or wherever the people are talking and listen to their opinions—whether positive or negative.

4. **Once you've measured, ACT!** Once you've measured the engagement of your workforce and come to understand the feedback they're giving you, *act on it*. It's not good enough just to say to them, "We're listening." Listening is an active process. Listening is adapting. Listening is coming up with new and better ways to engage your employees.

5. **Communicate, communicate, communicate.** Communication has a positive impact across the board, but particularly where engagement is concerned. If an organization has an open, communicative culture that fosters collaboration and respectful dialogue from the top down, the workforce will emulate this attitude. If an organization pays lip service to the idea of communication without fostering communication, the workforce will sniff this out as disingenuous. Encourage communication not just between those of equal ranks, but up and down the chain as well.

Chapter Five

Teamwork Today:
Fostering Collaboration

THE concept of collaboration shouldn't be foreign to anyone, least of all anyone involved in attaining and maintaining a strong, objective-oriented workforce. People have been collaborating in a working capacity for hundreds of years—we're talking way back to hunter/gatherer society, here. No man is ever truly an island, not even a self-employed man, and so collaboration is alive and well in all types of working environments.

However, there is a unique aspect to collaboration today, and that's the remoteness of the worker, or the potential remoteness of the worker. Due to changes (and advances, as some of these are absolutely positive things) in how workplaces are set up and how positions are envisioned and incented (such as telecommuting, flex-time, compressed work schedules, etc.), HR technology will need to change to take that into account. Not only are remoteness and flexibility themselves an aspect of the change, but also even *within* the office space, workers are thinking differently about collaborative spaces and opportunities. Workers for the most part, are no longer sitting in one place all day waiting for the phone to ring and taking occasional breaks to go to the bathroom, go outside for some fresh air, or hit the watercooler or lunchroom for some gossip. Younger workers in particular are used to a different type of collaboration in an anytime, anywhere sense using flexible, real-time technologies (being able to "like" a link instantly on Facebook, for instance) or the ability to chat/interact in real-time with peers. Thus, the need to mimic that sort of collaboration, or at least foster it, has changed into a requirement for the traditional workplace.

Harking back to our discussion on engagement, part of what undeniably motivates and engages people in an important social way is the concept of community interactions and communication. This is not to say that all workers are going to socialize and slack off given the chance, but rather to acknowledge the fact that communication is a part of human nature, and a valuable part of that nature as well. In order to keep your workers happy and engaged, you'll want to foster communication through collaboration.

The interpersonal relationships will bolster collaboration in the work sense, moving well beyond the social, very nearly monetizing the bonds that can happen in the workplace. Greater engagement leads to greater productivity leads to greater bottom lines. It also leads to an alignment of corporate practices with corporate goals. A company that purports to want to communicate with, collaborate with, listen to, and understand its customers, vendors and external colleagues needs to practice what it preaches.

With today's technologies, fostering true real-time collaboration has never been easier. But, like many of the other advances we've talked about in this book, the impetus for properly grasping and utilizing that technology isn't always acted upon. And this is where the pain point is: Because of the accessibility and success of these tools in the day-to-day life of our workforce, using these tools in a business environment has moved from a "nice to have" perk to a must-have tactic for organizations to stay in alignment and to keep employees engaged.

Growing Pains: "Social"

There's an unfortunate contradiction, or at least pushback, within HR about one important aspect of collaboration. Here, of course, I'm talking about social media or social technologies. While on the one hand, HR has seen collaboration as part of its responsibility, there's the unmistakable truth that most of the profession is still reeling from the notion of allowing Facebook to be accessed from work. So to start, you have a profession that's supposed to be fostering collaboration, that claims to be fostering collaboration, but that's scared to death of a collaborative tool—or anything that even remotely resembles that tool (and yes, I do believe that Facebook or Facebook-like tools can be productive).

Another problem with this reticence is that the vendors who are creating and selling the software that is helping organizations move forward with collaboration these days almost always emphasize the social aspect, or at least dub the capabilities as "social." But most organizations haven't gotten around to the point of saying: "Wow, social's a good thing!" This is a shame. Social isn't a time-waster if it's used correctly. It doesn't deserve the reputation it has gotten: that it's just a place where you talk about what you had for lunch. It's a place where people can learn from each other, understand who the experts are in an organization, reach out to those experts, and get things done for customers and colleagues—much faster than they've been able to before.

So I've found that the term "social" is throwing people off, whether or not it's warranted. Really, all we mean by this is sort of a slang term for collaborative and interactional—and that's primarily how I try to refer to it.

Growing Pains: The New Worker

Another pain point that frequently comes up in my discussions with organizations—even technologically nimble ones—is one that results from the reimagining of the workplace itself. As we've gotten away from the idea of workers having to be at their assigned desks to work, and as organizations have stretched to a more global nature as well as a more flexible schedule, no longer sticking to a 9-to-5 routine, the need for (and the pains around) collaboration has grown.

One company that I worked with recently was a major computer software manufacturer out of San Francisco. This is a company where no one in the organization, not even the administrative support staff, can be considered a stranger to the possibilities of technology. To underscore the need for a collaborative strategy even further, almost 90 percent of this company's workforce was virtual—a high number, but definitely not a rare number nowadays. This means that the office space has been reimagined as more of a hub where people from different departments can come and plug in when they need to use the space, rather than the traditional office space, where entire departments were clustered together and the people sitting next to you were working on the same projects you were. The hub situation gives a bit of the social aspect of collaboration and communication, but the fact that the hub serves the individual worker, rather than any one department, wouldn't necessarily foster the necessary departmental collaboration.

Part of driving engagement in this new environment is to look at the old ways of creating community and collaboration and translating those methods to the new workplace. And this hasn't been, nor will it be, just HR's job to navigate. It's a larger question of who owns collaboration in an enterprise. Concerning technology specifically, HR might own a piece, the CEO might own a piece, and IT might own a piece of the puzzle, too. If all aspects of the organization are in alignment, then the ownership across roles won't create a problem. However, if the owners are operating in their own silos, the pieces of the puzzle will never fall into place—the technology won't be truly integrated after rollout, and collaboration won't happen. Or, even worse, collaboration might happen in entirely different ways across the organization, and be applied inconsistently. There might be eighteen philosophies driving how the same workforce is asked to use collaborative tools. That's a lot of ground that's being covered without getting any traction. If each segment of ownership is in alignment with the bigger picture, however, the productivity of the whole enterprise is sure to be on the uptick.

Bringing It All Together With Big Data

One of the salves for this pain that happens as a result of operating in silos is the capacity for innovation granted to us by another buzzword, big data. It is estimated that 2.5 quintillion bytes of data are created each day. One of the primary reasons for this is because there's a constant flow of data now that gets generated by some of this flexible, remote collaboration: Chats, emails, text messages, and so forth. And organizations are just now starting to figure out how this data might be useful to them, grappling with how to run reports on what employees are talking about, what managers are dealing with, and how engagement is being broadcast across interpersonal and corporate communications. I think that some people misinterpret both the motives and the methodology behind this data collection, accusing organizations that practice it of implementing "Big Brother" tactics and watching over employees with eagle eyes. And I don't want to speak for every organization here, but I can say that most organizations are using this opportunity for good rather than for anything sinister. They are looking, correctly, at how to use this collaborative data to first, drive engagement, and second, understand what their workforce is thinking by getting the pulse of the sentiments being expressed.

Other than giving organizations a way to tap into the chatter that might help them from any number of standpoints, this big data collection (and the resulting dissemination) can be used to facilitate knowledge transfer—one of the vital components of proper succession management within business. The importance of this can't be overstated: When you think about the fact that somewhere between 30 to 50 percent of organizations today are going to have large chunks of their workers retiring in the next five or six years, the amount of accumulated knowledge that will walk out the door with them if not properly retained is staggering. But if we use the collaboration tools at our disposal properly, and find ways to analyze the data we capture, that accumulated knowledge isn't lost forever: We can instead use it to make the rest of the organization smarter. We'll be able to grow instead of shrink along with our numbers.

Tools for Collaboration

The tools that an organization can use are varied, and grow every day with the proliferation of apps and software geared toward collaboration and productivity in particular. When we talk about tools for collaboration, we could be talking about anything from a Facebook-like tool, where a manager can post what's going on today within

Jason Averbook 2014©

your department or division (think of SharePoint by Microsoft or Chatter by Salesforce.com, popular tools of this ilk) or even what's going on with them in their personal world on an internal basis rather than with the outside world. Team members can comment, share data and links, and collaborate from wherever they might be at the time, whether it's sipping a latte in another country or situated in one of the standard office cubes.

Text messaging offers an already built-up, standard method of collaboration. In instances when an email might be ignored and a phone call might take too much time, text messaging between employees allows a real-time flow of question and answers and concise information sharing. While not all of this chatter may be useful, even the "extraneous" chatter can be viewed as serving the larger purpose of creating a workplace with porous walls rather than concrete barriers to collaboration. Great work doesn't get done in a vacuum, and that goes for everyone.

Another example of a good use of collaboration is attaching a collaborative record to an employee record. Most organizations already have employee records—tomes of data on performance, basic data on salary and responsibilities, etc. If this record already exists, and we don't think of it in a silo or stovepipe but rather as part of a larger living, breathing document to encapsulate everything about that employee from residence to engagement, then adding collabora-tive records to that existing file isn't much of a stretch at all. Were this to be implemented, managers could easily access records of the chats they've had with that employee, pertinent topics, customer feedback and helpful comments that have been filtered through the employee, spots to work on (either in the business at large or with the employee in particular), and more. This is already happening on the customer level with customer relationship management (CRM) tools that allow employees across an organization to access detailed customer records. If we are aligning our internal practices with our external practices, implementing this sort of record-keeping with our employees is the next logical step. When we do this, we can make simple moments into moments that matter, feeding them into the larger collection of data and looking for trends, important points, and areas that are crying out for strategic intervention.

A Note on Policy

I'm not going to dwell on the issue of social media/collaboration policy or remote working too much in this chapter, because honestly, those topics could be their own book. But it's important to note that what ultimately makes flexible work environments successful—and work environments in today's knowledge economy in general, also—is having a collaborative culture and infrastructure built into the organization. It's not enough to pay lip service to the idea of collaboration and flexibility, rolling out a tool here or there, but then stifling your workforce's use of that tool or their desire to collaborate.

PR and marketing professionals deal with this kind of hard truth all the time: People are talking, whether you like it or not. The key to making the most of that chatter is to be a part of the conversation so that you can guide it, watch over it, and use it to your advantage. You don't want to create a culture where your employees keep their mouths shut until happy hour, when the chatter can turn destructive and put up a barrier to further engagement. If collaboration is not encouraged at a non-technical level, when you get to the technology—be it Facebook or Chatter or text messaging or whatever the tool may be—it's absolutely going to fail. If you have a social media or flexible work arrangement policy that truly reflects your values, and those values have been properly communicated to your workforce, those policies will ultimately be a success. But if you have policies in place that give mixed messages or the message wasn't communicated clearly in the first place, this will no doubt be at the root of your problems.

As I noted earlier, while the technology may have changed around collaboration, the fundamentals should be the same. The discussion about inappropriate versus appropriate behavior is not completely reconfigured just because we're talking about different tools like Facebook. Misbehaving on social media isn't any different than telling an off-color joke at a company function, misusing company time by taking an extra-long lunch break, or accessing inappropriate material on a work computer. Using Facebook and other social/collaborative tools properly is simply another extension of workplace responsibility and accountability and if you want to attract the best and the brightest employees—particularly from Generations Y and Z—you're going to need to offer them an environment where they can take a moment to check their Facebook, or take a moment to look at their email. The kinds of workers who need to be monitored on these tools are not the kinds of workers you'd want in your organization, anyway—and certainly, the brilliant, collaborative types aren't going to want to be in a culture where they're going to be stifled in what's come to be seen as somewhat of a personal right.

Collaboration needs to be a top-down venture. Like the alignment that I've promoted in other areas of HR leadership and corporate culture, collaboration is no exception. The executives

> Using Facebook and other social/collaborative tools properly is simply another extension of workplace responsibility and accountability.

in any organization need to show that they are willing to collaborate and willing to receive ideas, feedback, and even criticism. An organization full of leaders that encourage engagement and make themselves available to engage with is an organization well on the way to implementing collaboration and collaborative tools in the absolute best possible way. Collaboration is most nearly viral—seeing others collaborate will stoke the flames of one's own collaborative instincts, one's own curiosity, one's own desire to learn and grow as an employee and person.

Takeaways: Teamwork Today

1. **Collaboration can happen using remote technology just as much as face-to-face.** Today's workforce needs and the technology that's been made to support those needs are changing at a rapid rate. The way that we think of "face time" in the office and the way that we think of telecommuting for workers who may need or want to work remotely should change along with these shifting realities.

2. **Social tools aren't a luxury, nor are they time-wasters.** Because of how accessible, successful, and widely recognized social and social-like tools are, they have become a must-have in today's successful, agile workplace. These tools help employees stay engaged, aligned, productive, and open for communication in today's whenever, wherever world. Stop thinking of social media as a place to discuss the latest celebrity exploits. Social media is an awesome space, one built for sharing, learning, and communicating expertise (not to mention collecting data).

3. **Build a knowledge bank of collaborative data to ensure seamless succession down the line.** Consider the fact that somewhere between 30 to 50 percent of the workplaces today will be experiencing large volumes of retirement in the next few years. That's a lot of knowledge that can't be regained once it has walked out the door wearing a gold-plated watch. Use the collaboration tools, particularly the social ones, available now to aggregate data borne of meaningful collaboration as a knowledge

bank for your employees, especially those you have identified in your succession plan. You'll be glad you did.

4. **Keep things on the record—the employee record.** A useful place to store much of this data on collaboration is the employee record. Most organizations already have these for each employee, and they can include everything from new hire paperwork to ongoing performance reviews to complaints to commendations. If the employee record includes collaboration and communication collected throughout the employee's tenure, it becomes more of a living, breathing document that gives context to each employee across the organization.

5. **Good employees will always be good employees.** Don't let your fear of what can happen on social media sites keep you from advancing with the rest of the world. An employee making an inappropriate Facebook post is no different than an employee making an off-color comment at a company function. The best employees are generally going to be responsible, and the best employees these days are also ones who want to be able to have access to their social tools.

Chapter Six

Making Heads Count:
Measuring the Value of People

ONE of the things that HR has tried to be good at over the decades is counting heads. This means exactly what it sounds like, by and large; HR is the repository for all the information about the employee pool in an organization. When HR is using a "counting heads" philosophy, it's collecting the basic information: Names, Social Security numbers, and addresses—what it needs to get people paid. And it shouldn't surprise you that I advocate doing more.

When I give people advice on this topic, I'm using phraseology I cribbed from my mentor, Row Henson, while at PeopleSoft. I'll never forget her saying that the Holy Grail of HR is to shift from counting heads to making heads count, and that we're missing out if we can't find it. Oftentimes, when I sit with clients today, I'll hear that they don't even have a way to properly count their people, including contractors and employees, so they can't fathom using that human capital to drive a business advantage. This isn't good enough.

> The Holy Grail of HR is to shift from counting heads to making heads count.

What HR needs to do to ensure success—and not just for an individual department, but also for the organization as a whole—is to organize a strategic shift away from a philosophy that measures people by the numbers rather than making those individuals count for something. This means focusing on different data, and using that data to understand outcomes and strategy. This means truly tracking people, successfully measuring the outcomes of engagement and collaboration, and not just through the lens (or, more accurately, a mirror) of HR itself. These measurements should be taken within the context of the larger organization to continuously help promote alignment.

One of my favorite contrasts (and one which I've mentioned before in this book) between the philosophies of counting heads versus making heads count comes to the fore when looking at time to fill, meaning how long it takes an HR department to fill an open position. If, as an HR department, you're simply counting heads, you'll measure time to fill as if looking in a mirror. The number of days it takes to fill a position becomes about how long it took the HR department to get someone through the door and out on the other side of the paperwork process. But if you're looking at it from the perspective of making heads count, you'll want a more holistic understanding of why the time to fill metric is important. How much productivity, in dollars, does having that position unfilled for each day lose? Per week? Per month? How much does that compound, when looking at the larger organization—meaning how much stress does it cause the department where the vacancy is, what's the slowdown on shipping product, etc.?

Other than time to fill, some common examples of metrics measured by the HR department within an organization are:

✓ What training classes are offered and how many employees take advantage of them?

✓ What percentage of employees have returned open enrollment packets to access benefits?

✓ How many people in the organization have taken more than ten (or insert your personal number of concern here) days off?

✓ What is the attrition rate?

✓ What's the average cost of benefits per person?

This list can go on and on, of course, depending upon the needs of the organization, or what metrics each organization measures. There's not necessarily a standard set of metrics and there's no technology that you can purchase that will show you what you "should" be measuring. There's no standard scorecard. It's wonderful to gather information; I'm always advocating that organizations know their people as best they can. But it's not enough to simply get this information and keep it on file. It needs to *mean* something and have action tied to it. And in order for these measurements to mean something, there are a few things that need to be happening.

Getting Meaning From
Your Measurements

The absolute first and foremost thing that has to happen for your measurements and metrics to actually mean something is that they must be aligned to whatever the corporate or organizational goals and objectives are. If you're spending time measuring something that has nothing to do with the overarching goals of the organization, then you're basically collecting and reporting on meaningless data. There's nothing to work toward or to work from. If a company's goal is to increase the amount of customers a certain department can serve, and you help achieve this by decreasing your time to fill, then that's wonderful. But if you're measuring time to fill with no end goal in mind, or if you have an end goal and you're not measuring the proper metric, then you're just spinning your wheels.

The second step is that these measurements and the information gleaned from them must be delivered to people who can actually do something about the issue at hand/do something productive and proactive with this information. If the information is kept inside the HR silo, used only to help the HR team come up with modeling and predictions to help their individual team's end goals, that's not

helping the business. To really effect change, the information has to be put in the hands of people who can really do something with it. This doesn't mean that HR won't be involved in the final decision, or that HR needs to get defensive about getting credit for the information they collect—that's not helping anyone get things done. Getting things done ensures that the doers get a place at the table.

Finally, there must be prescriptions tied to the information. These measurements and data cannot just speak for themselves. The people who collect the data must analyze it. As an HR leader, the role should be to not just gather the information, but to deliver it with prescriptive action items that can be implemented, or at least considered, by the decision makers.

Easier said than done, perhaps.

Where, and What, *Is* the Data?

This may seem like a given, but I don't want you to take this for granted. One of the first things that needs to be in place when measuring the value of people, or measuring the value of *anything*, for that matter—and understanding how to prescribe impactful solutions—is a consistent, reliable, and logical flow of data. In order to make anything of these measurements, we have to know where the data sits. And unfortunately, most HR departments don't typically have their data stored in one place, and therefore can't pull it out and analyze the data in a way that makes sense.

I mean this in quite the literal sense. If I were an HR department run as those departments are typically run nowadays, I might have recruiting data stored in one system, basic employee information in another, logs of classes taken by each employee in yet another system, and so on. What this means is that when the time comes to run a report, there's not any easy way to break this information down or restructure it for my needs. If I wanted to know where I recruited people from and also have that correlated to how long they stayed with the company, I might not be able to find that in one fell swoop. If I wanted to see performance ratings tied to number of professional development credits, it might not be possible.

In order to combat this disorganization, HR needs to have a master data strategy—a plan in place that allows them to get all the data in one easily accessible format and system such that they can then generate the information and achieve alignment, delivery, and prescriptive measures with that data. Part of the aim of this master data strategy is to reach *beyond* the borders of HR, breaking down those silos and stovepipes that we were talking about earlier, and linking HR's data collection to the entire organization. This way, the data collected and the measurements taken don't just originate from the HR function, but can stretch across the organization as a whole, making true alignment and prescriptions a real possibility. For example, if we wanted to measure recruitment and cross-reference real-time sales data for those who were recruited from one place, we could do that using

Jason Averbook 2014©

a master data strategy with longer arms than those that only concern the HR function. The ultimate point here is that even if the data has served its supposed "purpose" from an HR standpoint—which is a good starting point, to be sure—that doesn't mean that it has served its purpose as far as the entire organization is concerned. And if our goal is alignment, then we're not going to achieve that goal looking at only data that helps the HR function.

I once worked with the head of HR for a casino. One of the interesting things about that particular industry, especially for someone like me who consults primarily in the HR space, is that almost everything that can "go wrong"—from restaurants, shops, the casino floor—is related to people. This forward-thinking HR leader said to her employees that she wanted all of the customer comment cards to come to her first, rather than being filtered through employees and then put into reports. This allowed her to see directly what issues customers were having with which employees in which departments. Because all of the data on these employees—across and among different departments—was stored in one place, she was able to look at a high-level overview and really understand where the problem areas were. If she had been unable to compare and correlate those measurements with other data points, she wouldn't have been able to manage and prescribe solutions nearly as effectively.

Finally, to really make this data work, it's important that the footwork be done to really understand what it is we *want* to measure, and that the people implementing the measurements systems understand what those goals for measurement are as well. This falls under the subheading of breaking down (or through) those silos, and working under a more holistic goal with other departments (the IT department in particular) to make sure that the tools fit the needs of HR. Even if we go through millions of dollars and millions of hours implementing new systems to gather and analyze data, if we aren't clear from the beginning about what it is we want to measure, how we want to correlate these measurements, and what we actually want to run impact analysis on, it's not likely that the end product is going to be able to give us what we want. It's like asking for directions without knowing your destination; what good will it do you to hope that your guide is a mind reader?

Or, we could put it another way: Imagine that you were undertaking a weight loss regimen, and you wanted to measure your weight out to three decimal points and commissioned a custom scale for the job. But you failed to communicate your needs properly to the engineer designing your scale, and when you received your measurement device, it only measured out to the pound. While many people would feel perfectly fine about seeing their weight measured to the pound, this didn't fit with what you had in mind when you embarked on this journey. If you don't know what you want to measure before you build something—or accurately communicate that need to the person who builds your tools—you're not likely to have the right kinds of measurements when your tools actually go live.

Making Measurement Happen

If you—or your IT department—are balking at the notion of a master data management strategy, thinking that it's just too massive to contemplate and implement, you're not alone.

But that doesn't mean that you're correct.

It's important to understand the distinction between having one *system* to use for everything and one *place* to store everything. I'm advocating the latter. To have one system to measure, analyze, and report all of your data isn't going to happen, unless you've got unlimited time and an unlimited budget and unlimited developers (and even the largest companies can't boast all of those things), and even then, not a great idea.

Understanding and implementing a master data management strategy will help move the focus away from rolling out modules and toward rolling out processes that enable data to flow from place to place. This is the first step to making sure that all data is stored and accessible in a way that it's actually useful to the organization.

To address the second pain point we talked about in this chapter—not having a truly complete set of data—we must make sure that there's an enterprise strategy for the creation of some sort of data warehouse in the organization. What this means is that HR data and other data are stored at a central point, making everything easy to cross-reference.

To solve the problem of our tools not fitting the job, it's as simple as making sure that the engineers understand from a business standpoint what questions they'll need to design their tools to answer. HR needs to bridge the gap between the business and IT, translating what intelligence would be helpful to the overarching organization and making sure that IT can make the gathering and reporting of this intelligence happen. You can see how this would be impossible for HR to achieve on its own—there needs to be some major reaching across the aisle here. To facilitate this, HR needs to understand what language the business speaks, rather than the language that HR speaks.

Takeaways: Making Heads Count

1. **Focus on more than just the data.** Your measurements should be looked at from a high-level organizational point of view, rather than just from an HR standpoint. The data that comes from these measurements must be understandable and truly measure important outcomes.

2. **Align yourself.** No matter what you're measuring, all of your metrics must be aligned to whatever the organizational objectives are. If this doesn't happen, and if there isn't a strategy behind what you're measuring, those metrics will essentially be meaningless.

3. **Deliver your measurements to people that matter.** This isn't to say that there are people in the organization that *don't* matter, but you should always be delivering your data specifically to those who can actually do something with that information. If you've put all this work into strategy and aligned measurements only to deliver them to a person or department who can't act on the information, all your work will be for naught.

4. **There must be prescriptions tied to the information.** It's not enough to collect data. While data is good, actionable items are better. Analyze the data that you collect, and when you deliver it to the individuals who can do something with it, make sure that there are prescriptive solutions outlined in the report for the decision makers to implement—or at the very least, consider.

5. **Get organized.** You know how all the socks might be in different drawers, and not paired up? And you know how long it takes you to get ready in the morning because of that? Data management is a little like that. In order to combat disorganization—and lack of action—HR needs to have a master data management strategy in place allowing it to access all data in one system. This allows any user to generate information, achieve alignment, and initiate action with that data.

Chapter Seven

Helping the Workforce Work Better and Faster: Deploying Cloud-Based Technology

ULTIMATELY, when we have these big picture discussions about collecting data, running reports, and implementing solutions based on analysis of those reports, we're really talking about people, process, AND technology. Technology is the connective tissue, the crux of the thing. While without the proper end goals in mind, we can't put in place the proper technology. T6he notion of properly deployed technology is still essential to the success of the modern organization.

At a certain point, it would have been fair to say that the biggest problems with the deployment of technology were the logistical issues presented by things like hardware speed and software delivery methods. Companies historically had not been able to push technology out to their people in a consistent, simple, or cost-effective manner. But as bandwidth has improved and technology has continued to advance, now being delivered by the cloud, it has given the technology implementers and decision makers the ability to begin to better solve that problem, pushing technology out where it needs to go in a more consistent, simple, and cost-effective manner.

It would have been also been safe to venture that the software wasn't the only problem with deployment of technology in the past— the hardware was more difficult to come by, too. Cumbersome

mainframe computers and even early personal computing sta-
tions could be cost-prohibitive and certainly didn't translate to a
very nimble network. But today, there are new opportunities to
be online anywhere, anytime. In fact, most people *are* online anywhere, anytime, thanks to the ever-present "cloud." A report on
disruptive technologies delivered by the consulting firm McKinsey & Company in May of 2013 succinctly notes that: "With cloud
technology, any computer application or service can be delivered
over a network or the Internet, with minimal or no local software
or processing power required."

This means that consumers themselves are able to have access
to unprecedented technology in a mobile format—tablets, smartphones, netbooks, etc. Everyone is using this technology ("The
cloud is enabling the explosive growth of Internet-based services,"
notes McKinsey in the same report), whether it be employees in a
retail store in the break room, customers at a hotel restaurant at the
table, or people who are sitting down with their spouse at home to
try to figure out their benefits package.

So it's definitely true that the software and hardware are no
longer the primary culprits in the workplace. Now, like many of
the other pain points discussed in this book, the problems surrounding technology as it relates to HR can be attributed to the
fact that the technology has been looked at almost as a segregated
set of tools built to strictly serve the HR function. This, of course,
is at odds with the kind of alignment that promotes success. In
order for the technology to be of any utility to its users, it needs to
be conceived, written, and available in the language of those users,
rather than in the language of someone simply entering data into
the tool. If the tool is only usable to an HR expert, then it will fail
right out of the gate.

"I am not filling this out for HR!"

Jason Averbook 2014©

This knowledge, in addition to the unprecedented availability of nimble, cloud-based technology, makes for one of those perfect storms of opportunity and innovation that I'm so fond of. Where others see challenge, I tend to see opportunity. I'm hoping that, by this point, you feel the same way.

Why Change, Why Now?

Other than embracing change for the sake of it, there's a very good reason why HR managers and other professionals should be investing in new technological strategies and tools. Primarily, this is because when organizations do this, they give employees, managers, and executives the opportunity to engage in what I call *the magic three:*

✓ Push
✓ Pull
✓ Interact

What I mean by the first peg of this triumvirate is pretty clear—we've been doing this for a while now throughout industry. When we *push*, we push information to people and let them consume it. We aren't necessarily guiding them, or telling them how to consume the information or which information to consume, but we're pushing it out, hoping that it's magically arriving at a time when the recipients need the information and can actually get some use from it.

When we *pull*, I'm not talking about us in the C-suite pulling anything. Rather, this second part means that we've structured a system such that the employees, managers, or executives in an organization can pull information when they need it—also known as a just-in-time intelligence. This approach assumes that these end users are comfortable enough with the technology to be able to pull information, pull reports, and run certain types of searches when they need it. When the systems are well designed, this is, in fact, more than wishful thinking!

The third peg is extremely important, and particularly exciting for me. When I say *interact*, I'm talking about a form of collaboration: really interacting with the technology to truly become more productive in the workplace by collaborating with others, modeling, and planning. If I'm interacting with the technology to answer pertinent questions—such as, "If I give everyone a 3 or 4 percent increase, what does that do to my overall budget?" or "If I allow these certain employees to take this day off, what does that do to my schedule?"—then I'm able to really make use of the technology as a decision-making tool.

Interacting is really the ultimate goal here; it encompasses both push and pull. And now we have the opportunity to really interact. It hasn't always been this way; up until the last few years, all employees have been able to do is *push* data to the HR or payroll departments. And here when I say data, I mean, of course, paper. Mountains and mountains of paper would accumulate and bottleneck at the HR or payroll desks, and the people manning those desks would have to focus on entering data. Since these employees were probably concerned with their productivity above the interests of the larger business, either by mandate or by inertia, they would start to streamline their own process, leaving out certain data points and only entering the bare minimum necessary to get employees paid and to keep the lights on. This may save time in the moment, but it ends up causing a lot of pain down the line with a huge opportunity cost—especially, as we've talked about, when people who allegedly represent our most valuable asset have to repeat their name ten times each day on different forms for the first month or so of employment.

So it's only recently that maybe, if truly thought through, we've had a rich enough data set to really work with and measure value, making heads count. And it's only recently that, due to the cloud, we've been able to more seamlessly push out the technology that makes the collection and analysis of this kind of data possible. In the past, delivery of systems and updates were so slow (and physically different) that they were jokingly referred to as "sneaker net"— meaning the only way to get a software update on your computer was for an IT person in sneakers to physically come to your workstation with a CD-ROM to install the technology onto the computer. And the only way for IT people to get the technology was for it to be physically sent through the mail. (Remember the famous America

Online CDs? Do you have a few still lying around your house? They make excellent coasters!) Now, sneaker net is no more; we're truly immersed in the Internet, and it makes good on the name. In fact, the hardware has changed to reflect the fact that most software comes from the cloud—tablets have never had a slot for CDs/DVDs, and many laptops are now created without that capability. Because of what the cloud brings to the world, you don't need those inputs. Now, we can distribute and consume technology in a truly seamless, effortless way. We get updates from the app store or pushed to us from the cloud when an update is available, as opposed to having to wait for the sneaker net to come around to our desks.

The expectation of the workforce has changed accordingly. Now that they're getting technology served up to them on a minute-by-minute, second-by-second basis and they're used to consuming technology this way (both as employees and consumers), it places new challenges on the HR function. It's now time for HR to rei-magine how they push out the technology and services to people as well as how they get those same people to truly interact with the technology such that they can then add value to the organization.

There couldn't be a better opportunity to make this happen. There couldn't be a better time than now.

What's in It for Me?

One unfortunate side effect of moving from the "sneaker net" model to a more responsive, real-time model of technology is that employ-ees seem to have the perception that they're now being asked to do HR's job. So in addition to the myriad of things that the typical employee now has to do in this economy of more-with-less, she is worried that she has to deal with the paperwork that, in the past, she would have typically been able to push onto HR.

The notion that the HR of the past was a "full-service" model, whereas today it's asking employees to take part in "self-service," is just that—a notion. In order to enable efficiency and make the most of the changes happening in the space today, it's essential that the HR technology leaders embark upon a campaign to get employees to understand the benefits of the new tools. It's a process, to be sure, but the first step couldn't be simpler: Stop calling it "self-service!" Promote it as a more usable tool, a quicker tool, a tool of the people and for the people—but don't make it sound like your employees are going to have to stand at a gas station getting covered in grease and soot waiting to fill up their own tank. I advise clients to call this type of technology *direct access*—it sounds more positive, it's absolutely accurate, and it lets employees know that the power rests in their hands.

One of the most common acronyms we run into when talking about change enablement (sometimes called change management, but for the purposes of this book, we'll be sticking with change enablement) is WIIFM, or What's In It For Me? HR must stop asking this question as it relates to their own work and start anticipating what the answer should be when it's the employees who are asking. At every single turn, the HR bigwigs must put themselves in the shoes of the average worker, anticipating any resistance and truly understanding the benefits of the new tool when they begin to push it out to employees and managers. This is truly putting a different lens on things, making sure that you're considering the other side of the table.

To do this properly, I'd strongly suggest bringing employees and managers onto the project teams responsible for designing, selecting, and deploying new technology to assure that their interests are represented, they are invested, and WIIFM ultimately becomes a rhetorical question.

Jason Averbook 2014©

You'll also want to make sure that the types of technology that you're pushing out to your workforce are things that they will actually use on a frequent to semi-frequent basis. Think about the top transactions that HR has had to push out in the past in terms of your *own* life. How often have you changed your address? Had a child? Gotten married or divorced? These are major changes, but unless something entirely unusual happens, this probably isn't occurring every year. The chances that an employee will be able to remember to update their information or to even understand where and how to offer these updates are slim if the last time he used the technology was three or five years ago.

If we were to look at this through the lens of the HR department, we might see that eliminating the collection of all of those life events from the entire workforce would save us a lot of time and effort. But that's classic WIIFM on the HR side. It would be much more prudent to flip the question over, viewing it through the lens of the employee, thinking about what his needs are, how often he'll need to use the technology, what he needs to use it for, how it could make his life easier, and so on.

In a properly aligned workplace, the WIIFM becomes irrelevant. Employees understand that HR wants to roll out tools that are usable and useful. HR gains the efficiency of having employees who can truly interact with useful tools. And the organization runs smoother, works smarter, and does better.

The Cloud

One of the major developments that have helped to facilitate the transition from the sneaker net to the seamless delivery process is the cloud. Even if you're not an HR or technology professional, you've heard of the cloud—as a consumer of modern technology, you're probably already up there! On the HR/IT side, the cloud has helped to alleviate so much of the spending and resource allocation that had been taken up by physically implementing applications, storage servers, databases, and bandwidth typically associated with running an organization.

In the old school of thought, back in the on-premise software era, it was all too easy for HR to shrug and pass the buck, saying that they'd given IT their specifications and it was up to the IT department to work out how it would deal with the demands on its time, space, and technical skills. It was IT's job to deliver what HR had asked for. But now, in the world of the cloud, we've moved to a different sort of delivery model: **Software as a Service (SaaS).**

SaaS is a category of software that allows its administrators to push out updates to users in a fairly or completely seamless way. SaaS is most nearly defined as software that is owned or updated remotely, without any impact or onus on the user. Tools like LinkedIn and Facebook are SaaS tools, with each vendor releasing numerous updates *per day*. We as users don't know it when it's happening. We might hit the refresh button and find a new capability there that wasn't there a moment ago. Or, we might never notice a behind-the-scenes patch that makes things run a little more smoothly on the back end. In the old world of technology, this would require having everyone log out for a specified period of time—usually a few hours—while the installation of updates took place. Now, with SaaS, that lag time isn't just reduced, it's frequently gone altogether. SaaS allows developers to deploy more agile products that can evolve in rapid response to user needs.

The proliferation of SaaS also means that, just as HR has had to reframe how it selects and deploys software for the users, those same leaders must now reimagine how they work together with the IT function to select the software and tools that they need. Gone are the days when HR could just throw its requirements at IT and wait for a solution that might fit them. Now, HR has to select and lever-age this technology themselves, partnering now with vendors who design the SaaS tools, which can now be delivered more directly to an organization with less involvement from the middleman of IT.

In other words, in the cloud world, strategy and technology are no longer separate entities—they are one in the same, brought together by innovation and possibility.

I can't emphasize enough how valuable this increase in speed is for an organization. One client of mine, a major manufacturer, looked at its overall goals and knew that it needed a strategy that played to the strength of this speed. The executives wanted to make sure that managers had more control of approval processes for salary increases, time off, performance reviews, etc. The thought was that managers could save time and energy, and promote efficiency if they could do this in a way that would fit with their day-to-day jobs.

This was a case where the HR team was doing two very important things: First, the needs of the employees (managers) were considered, and second, the tools were selected with the overarching strategy in mind. We were able to roll out direct access capabilities for the managers, enabling them to do the things and have the insight they needed to be more productive and to do their jobs well. The SaaS we used automatically generated and sent a to-do list to managers which would then allow them to approve (or deny) in one fell swoop all the things they needed to review that day. And because of the anytime/anyplace nature of today's technology, it was what we call "device agnostic"—meaning they could do it from their desktop at work, their laptop on the road, their tablet from their living room. The list was delivered to them via email as well as a portal they were already using frequently, meaning they didn't need to log on to a separate application. A process that used to take eight to ten *days* to move through the organization, trailing a massive pile of paper in its wake, was now completed seamlessly and painlessly through the cloud in eight to ten *seconds*. Part of the beauty here is that SaaS allows organizations of all sizes to leverage the speeds and capabilities present in larger organizations without breaking the bank.

Not all companies have been so successful, however, and we can learn from their missteps. I've mentioned that one of the considerations that is particularly important when rolling out these types of solutions is that the solutions must be user-friendly, written in the language of the user, and applicable to that user's job. Even though this technology typically makes the jobs of those users easier, you're fighting the perception—and the reality—that sometimes, writing a bunch of information down on paper and sticking it in the interoffice mail is easier (on the surface) than logging into a tool, figuring out how to use that tool, and entering the information. When troubleshooting enters into the mix, the frustration will increase exponentially. This is a moment where employees might start to think of it as a self-service situation (read: gas station), rather than a direct access scenario.

One major technology firm I worked with learned this the hard way. They did a bi-annual performance review of all employees, first on paper and eventually through a newer piece of technology. The company was continually getting the feedback that managers and employees hated the process, and didn't see any value in it. Understandably, HR was quite frustrated with this sentiment, so they went out and purchased newer technology—something much sleeker and sexier. So the software looked better, but that's where the improvements ended. Nothing of any significance had changed, and so employees still didn't see the value in it, and still didn't use it. Three months after the company had rolled out its new tool, they called me to tell me that their employees refused to engage with it. I had to deliver the bad news that the problem wasn't with the technology, it was with the underlying process, and they needed to go back to the drawing board, seeing things from another angle and leaving their HR-colored glasses behind.

Likewise, sometimes implementing solutions can be time-consuming and costly without payoff. A major insurance company that I worked with decided to hop on board with Twitter and use the social media technology to be its center for recruitment. But Twitter being a fairly new technology at that time, the company didn't have a SaaS solution in place that would have accepted it cleanly. Rather, there was what we call an on-premise solution that IT was responsible for maintaining. The new mandate meant that IT had to spend a lot of time and money—to the tune of six months and $4 million—upgrading their recruiting applications to allow for integration with Twitter and Facebook, essentially retrofitting an expensive system that the company already owned. This is the opposite of agile. By contrast, if we were using a SaaS solution, we could have downloaded the app and integrated it painlessly. And every time the vendor has a new release of the software, the company would be able to take advantage of it without having to lean on IT to come and upgrade each machine individually.

Another advantage of SaaS technology is not only how scalable it is, but how configurable. In the past, in order to have software look and feel like I wanted it to, I would have to undertake some major customization—again leaning on IT, who were receiving instructions rather than operating from an inherent understanding of what I wanted to accomplish. Piles of code would have to be written, and piles of money would be burned up in the process. But like Facebook or LinkedIn, where individual consumers can configure their profile or home page, HR SaaS solutions have drop-down menus, checkboxes, and widgets that help organizations and individual users configure the programs to their needs. Whereas customization would cost untold amounts of money and time, configurability ensures functionality without rendering the software useless for the next user or the next department—particularly important in a time when many companies have a global presence, and what works for one geographic location might not logistically work for another (think simple here: Different places, different languages). Configurability is also umpteen times more wonderful than relying on customization, because as best practices change for each industry and department, users are able to be nimble and move with the changing tides.

Now that's agility.

Takeaways: Helping the Workforce Work Better and Faster

1. **If the tool is only usable to HR, it will fail.** Any tool deployed to the larger workforce needs to be written in the language of those who are using the tool. Quite often, specialized departments have their own specialized language, and that's fine if we're working in isolated stovepipes and silos. But that's not what we're after—we're after connectivity and collaboration across all departments. If a tool is meant for the larger population—and successful tools of the aligned workforce will be—then that larger population needs to understand how to use that tool.

2. **The Magic Three: Push, Pull, Interact.** Effective technology solutions should allow the workforce to push data, pull data, and interact with the data. In order for data to be viable, it must be accessible and interactive. By interacting with the data you collect, your organization can model and plan for various scenarios, rather than just experiencing them anew each time they arise.

3. **The cloud is agile.** The recent developments around cloud computing allow you to more seamlessly push out updates to technology and are more in tune with how the modern worker understands today's software. The cloud isn't going to cost you as much in overhead or in physical space—it's information housed elsewhere with greater flexibility and accounts for the rapid changes of today's workplace (and workforce).

4. **The workforce is full of tech-savvy consumers.** People are used to getting constant, seamless updates from SaaS solutions that they use in their day-to-day lives, such as Facebook and LinkedIn. This expectation is no different in the workplace.

5. **The cloud is cost-effective.** Whereas you used to have to spend money on hardware such as servers and software such as database licenses, the cloud allows you to make seamless updates in much less time, which equals much less money.

Chapter Eight

Owning IT:
Taking Charge of Technology

NOW, more than ever, technology is an indispensable part of our lives. Don't believe me? Where's your phone? How close do you sleep to your device? If you're anything like me, it's probably in your hand, buzzing intermittently as emails, texts, and notifications fly in from the ether, interrupting your train of thought while you're supposed to be reading. Put down the phone! I know, I know; chances are, you can't. Or you think you can't. This is all the proof I need.

But joking aside, there's an irony in all this indispensability, particularly in the workplace. I'm speaking about the fact that no matter how important we say technology is, in HR, often the responsibility of technology and the decisions surrounding what kind to employ and deploy are offloaded to the IT department. HR once looked at technology as an industry unto itself, and counted on someone else to make decisions about it, provide it, maintain it, and change it when necessary. HR didn't want to know what was in the sausage; they just wanted to eat it, blissfully ignorant of its components.

As our need for technology has evolved, so has the technology. We've talked about how SaaS has been a total game-changer, allowing for configurability and ease of updates like we've never seen before. And as we are all increasingly plugged in to technology, it

Jason Averbook 2014©

follows that we all have specific needs and functions that we desire technology to fulfill. This kind of specialization, combined with the advances in the technology itself, means that to sit back and wait for

IT to take charge is neither efficient nor desirable. Unfortunately, HR departments often continue to see it differently, choosing to see their job function as one that is separate from technology. The work of leveraging technology to make their lives easier is somehow not their job; generally, they would rather (or for some reason think they need to) tell IT what they need and hope that IT can either come up with something to fill that need or create it out of thin air.

When technology is developed and/or chosen this way, IT is simply bombarded with a list of tasks completely without context or reason. From IT's perspective, these tasks were just ingredients to a recipe it was blindly following, having no way to prioritize or contextualize those ingredients. They wouldn't know what was most important or least important to the department who had put in the request. They would have no idea why they were doing what they were doing, and how it may or may not align with the overarching goals of the business. They would only think: I need to get X amount of software ready and I promised it by Y date. This silo and stovepipe situation often results in very costly, very stiff (as opposed to agile) "solutions" that offer little in the way of a user-friendly, efficient, and aligned experience for the requesting department.

In the case of the HR–IT relationship, this has been historically detrimental, to say the least. A huge chasm between the function of HR and IT was created, often to the point of devolving to finger-pointing. If IT threw something over the fence that didn't meet the bar that HR felt they set, IT would get blasted for creating/purchasing software that "sucked." The notion that IT spoke only its own language was continually furthered by the fact that, oftentimes, left with no detailed direction, IT indeed had no other recourse than to choose vendors and applications that only spoke its language, rather than the language that HR was hoping for. Because there was no attention paid to the language of the overall organization, it's not surprising that this language barrier continued to develop. HR and IT, locked in a perpetual blame game, had been pushed into a standstill so venomous that even the vendors associated with the chosen software got their reputations sullied in the mix. That's a lot of negativity, and not a lot of forward motion.

At Your Service?

What this all led to was the repeated accusation by HR that they weren't getting support from IT (and vice versa). Knowing that IT's first priority is typically to complete the tasks that are going to give the organization a competitive advantage, followed by providing some back-end office support, it's not that wild of an accusation. The stovepipes and silos of an unaligned organization furthered conflicts stemming from these asymmetrical priorities. One solution that many intrepid organizations came up with was to create a Human Resource Information Systems (HRIS) function—sort of a hybrid between HR and IT. These groups were information service groups that worked within the function of HR, giving HR some control over software and solutions.

But unfortunately, hybridity can backfire. When someone in the HRIS function went off on their own, executing some program or process that worked from a technology standpoint, they were often too low on the totem pole of HR to understand what the HR function wanted. Conversely, if a product was working for the HR function, it might not fit with the overall IT/IS protocols. This quagmire was further confounded by the fact that the groups were often managed by HR pros (like compensation and benefits leaders), rather than IT experts, meaning that there was a conflict of interest in who the management reported to—their loyalties lay with compensation and benefits people, rather than IT. And it caused further fractures in the alignment of the organization as a whole, with HR seen as an unorthodox thorn in the side of IT goals for the organization.

The Bottom Line: You Can't Opt Out

Now that you've got some of the background, and perhaps can better understand some of the conflicts that are no doubt happening within the walls of your own organization, you probably see where I'm headed with all of this. The bottom line is that in today's world, where we're consumed by technology and technology is the best and frankly only way to get from now to next, HR can no longer opt out of the IT function. Technology shapes the expectation of every consumer, and this is true from within an organization—potential hires, managers, the workforce, recent retirees, and on and on. No matter what your role is in the organization, you've got to be comfortable becoming a technologist.

By becoming a technologist, I don't mean that you need to go back to school and obtain some kind of advanced degree, or that you need to be a programmer. But there is no longer separation of church and state between strategy and technology—in order to be successful, an organization must close the chasm between its strategic goals and the technology functions that allow it to achieve those goals. If you don't achieve this, you are and will forever be at a competitive disadvantage, locking yourself in a cycle of less-than-agile thinking and process.

In order for HR to accomplish this, every HR department must have a process and technology function incorporated into its goals and objectives. This should be a designated person or a team. This function, ideally, is constantly thinking about how the department's processes and technologies work together, how those processes and technologies are seen by employees and managers, and ultimately how those processes and technologies are seen and used by those employees and managers rather than by the HR function itself.

The team must also concern itself with staying up to date with the market as far as what's trending in technology. Technology, as you know, changes very quickly—by the month, even—and continuing to look at the market landscape is another full-time concern. Where and who are the vendors of today? Who will be the vendors of tomorrow? Which software platforms make the most sense for the organization's long-term efforts? Who is developing software platforms that most closely align with the organization's goals now, and in the future as well?

Lastly, these designated watchdogs need to focus on data. It's data that lets any employee, manager, or HR function have the flexibility and foresight to truly understand everything that's going on around them in the organization now and in the future. There needs to be a focus on the right kind of data—collecting that data, first of all—and then the right kind of reporting. There needs to be someone watching to make sure that there's one way to store data and use that data in the enterprise, and that the HR function always knows how to access that data, rather than relying on IT to run a report and toss it back over the fence. With the right kind of data and the right kind of reporting, HR can control its own destiny, rather than sitting on the sidelines waiting for updates to come to it from other arms of the organization. And this all goes back to helping build strategy around measuring workforce engagement, productivity, turnover, and all of those other important markers that go into the secret sauce of an organization's success.

This is a big shift for any organization, and the history surrounding the often seen as less-than-stellar HRIS efforts of the past have shown that if the shift is to truly be successful, it must be undertaken with complete integration in mind. It's not enough to toss an IT person into the HR mix and have them report solely to an HR leader. Nor is it enough to have an HR person hand-deliver missives to IT department meetings and call that integration. True, seamless integration and HR ownership of technology within its own function versus counting on IT is what's required. Having HR reimagine its own technologies and processes rather than counting on IT to reimagine those same technologies and processes without direction is what's required.

The other important thing to call out is that this process and technology function or team can't be seen as a low-level function on the totem pole. Rather, it must be seen as a function that sits at the table with HR leadership so that it can constantly see what HR is doing and thinking, as well as the goals that HR is trying to reach, so that the team can be fully aligned—not just in terms of strategy, but in terms of priorities as well.

There's Still a Place for IT

All that having been said, I want to be clear about something: There's still a place for IT. This rallying cry doesn't mean that I'm implying that HR step in and fulfill the IT function. Rather, I mean that HR must think of IT truly as the supporting function rather than the doing function, and IT must think of itself that way, in turn. Inevitably, friction can happen when another department begins to "involve itself" in technology, using IT parlance; but in order for this alignment to be successful, IT has to realize that in today's technology-saturated world, it's impossible for any department, no matter how far removed from the technology function, to stay out of the technology mix. Just because something has to do with technology, it doesn't automatically mean that it's purely an IT responsibility—that's how we got into this spot in the first place.

Specifically, HR needs assistance from IT in three big areas. The first is making sure that all the technology that HR is using is completely integrated into the larger enterprise. This is a perfect place for IT to help out. By leveraging their expertise on networking and systems, IT can help ensure that data capture and storage is useful to the entire organization, rather than just HR.

By doing so, the IT department can assist in the second area, which is to ensure that the HR department isn't purely storing names in its own silo over in HR, and that everywhere else in the organization, there's seamless access to employee records across the board. This ensures that if I'm a salesperson in an organization and I'm entered on my hire paperwork as Jason Averbook that I'm always going to be "discoverable" as Jason Averbook, and not spread out across the system as J. Averbook or Averbook, J. It seems simple, but it's by no means a given, and it can really throw a kink into not only alignment, but the perception that employees are actually valued assets with names, faces, and individual roles.

The third area where IT can really shine deserves a book all on its own, and that's security. There must be standards for any and all enterprises when it comes to the security of their data, and this is something that absolutely falls under the purview of IT. Not only must internal security be a priority, but now, in the age of the cloud and SaaS, the vendors used to store and process data must be closely examined as well. These standards are always complex and sometimes regulated by law (such as in finance), and should be applied to the organization as a whole, rather than just the HR function.

So even in this brave new world where we're all technologists, IT has a big role, and without IT, HR will surely fail. It's important not to overcorrect on the issue of becoming a technologist, although it's definitely tempting with the ease of use that we can typically find in SaaS technologies. While it's true that vendors are deploying easier-to-use technologies nowadays, you still want to avoid any kind of thinking that separates IT and HR, or HR and any department, into silos.

Competencies for the HR Process and Technology Group

When it comes to thinking about the competencies that are required for the ideal HR process and technology group, I see them falling into six key areas. It's fair to say that each area could be its own job, but depending upon the budget and structure of your organization, they may be integrated into one person or a few people. Again, there's never a silver bullet here—it's all about what works best for you.

Jason Averbook 2014©

#1: The Process Ninja

The Process Ninja is someone who is constantly thinking about process, and who brings experience in this area to the table. In the industry, we have what are called Six Sigma Black Belts—people who have gone through Six Sigma training and have a complete understanding of process efficiency. While not everyone will have access to such highly-trained specialists, it's fair to say that every HR function needs someone who thinks broader than just about a single problem at once; rather, that person should be thinking about how processes interact with one another, how they work to solve recurring problems or problems that have exponential implications, and so on.

#2: The Strategic Functional Analyst

Commonly referred to, also, as a Business Analyst, this person takes the ideas and requirements of HR and its workforce and

Jason Averbook 2014©

maps out what needs to happen in order for those ideas and requirements to align with the corporate goals and objectives, all through the lens of understanding how to turn that alignment into usable technology. This person is really a coffee filter, as it were, that makes the technology view usable to the non-technology view and vice versa. Specifically, the Functional Analyst and the Process Ninja are trained to translate between the two lenses of HR and IT.

Jason Averbook 2014©

#3: The User Experience Expert

The third important role is someone whose scope of practice focuses on user experience. In this case, the consumer is the employee, the manager, or the workforce at large. This person thinks about which user interfaces, which vendors, and which software best fit the need of the department or employee requesting it. Another important role for this person is to focus on how the overall experience (people, process, and technology) is for the employee and manager, and get away from focusing on deploying modules and instead focus on deploying processes to the workforce.

Jason Averbook 2014©

#4: The Change Enablement/Marketing Ace

This role is a beautiful bridge from now to next. In many (un-aligned) organizations, change enablement (or change management) is oftentimes handled by a corporate communications or training department. The former will inform employees about new policies and procedures, while the latter (often outsourced) will bore employees to tears while sapping time away from the typical workday.

This normally results in a lot of jargon and a lot of money left on the table. I worked with a major government contractor who rolled out a learning management system (LMS) and worked with their corporate communications team to come up with a program to get the employees to use the new LMS. They created a bunch of posters to hang up around the halls with a race car and a tagline underneath inviting the employees to come kick the tires of the new LMS. On the poster, they actually used the acronym LMS. Can you guess how many employees came around to kick the tires? Almost zero. Can you guess why? They didn't know what an LMS was! This is a classic example of departments using internal language that means nothing out of context—another thing that happens when alignment isn't top of mind. The change enablement person needs to be thinking about that What's In It For Me ideology that's so pervasive in the workplace and the world in general—acting as a translator, letting the workforce know how the new tools will benefit them in the now and in the next.

#5: The Workforce Intelligence (the Data Czars)

In the workforce intelligence role, what we're looking for is someone who is responsible for thinking about how to provide data to the consumers (who might be employees, managers, executives, HR people, etc.) in a consistent manner. This doesn't tend to happen on its own; it's not as common as one would hope.

Case in point, I worked with a major healthcare organization where the CEO had summed up his problem thusly: "I could ask five people in HR how many employees we have working in this organization, and I could get five different answers." That struck me as odd. Shouldn't a concrete fact—number of employees—be a concrete answer? It turned out that the reason why this was happening in this case, and the reason it happens in other cases, is two-fold. People interpret the question differently, first of all, and secondly, they pull that data from different sources that often haven't been integrated or aligned with one another.

This role, then, looks at being able to create one source of true information. And creating that source begins with technology, but also with process—making sure there's a consistent way to measure each metric (headcount, in this case).

#6: The Technologist

This sixth role is the role of the technologist itself—one who does nothing but think about the market, keep abreast of the tech-

nology solutions available, and keep alignment with the organization in mind. This person understands what enterprise technology tools are available, what is needed from an HR standpoint, and works closely with both HR and IT groups to make decisions about what technology to purchase and deploy.

What often happens is that an IT department

will go out and license a piece of technology such as CRM software, bringing that technology in-house. But then, soon thereafter, HR will come up with an idea about what the organization needs—a call center or a service center, for example—without knowing that the CRM software they have already offers that capability (and has already been paid for—to the tune of quite a bit of money). If the technologist were on the lookout, the organization could have saved a lot of time, money, and effort, as well as caused a lot less confusion, by not purchasing a duplicate tool.

• • • •

Ultimately, how your team looks will depend upon your organization's budget, capabilities, and goals. Always, always goals. Remember that, as with anything else, if you approach the end game with strategy in mind—or use strategy for your foundation, however you prefer to see it—your results will be in alignment and foster further alignment. If you draw the right roadmap, you'll be able to find your way, but you can't draw the right roadmap without knowing where you're going in the first place.

Takeaways: Owning IT

1. **We are all technologists now.** No matter what our role is in our organization, we can't offload technology tasks entirely to IT. We all must be conversant in technology.

2. **HR departments must have process and technology continuously on the brain.** The more that those in the HR space can think about which processes and technologies can be put in place to support what they're trying to accomplish, the better. IT isn't going to be able to see what HR needs from the inside; only HR can truly understand these needs. If HR has tech on the brain, then it will be easier to translate those needs to IT.

3. **It's the job of HR, not IT, to reimagine its processes.** HR should clearly communicate its strategy, goals, and objectives to IT when asking IT to design or assist with the purchase of a tool, rather than simply give IT a punch list of "must-haves."

4. **Without IT, HR will surely fail.** The answer is not to blame IT or to try to exclude them from the process. In today's world, there's no way to move forward without technology, and without IT to help facilitate the use of that technology.

5. **The prescription for success: a six-pronged process and technology group.** To avoid cannibalizing priorities from one side of the table or the other, it's best to have a group of employees who can wear both lenses—who think of HR with IT in mind and vice versa.

Chapter Nine

The Five Things You Need to Succeed

FIRST things first—I'd like to offer a bit of a disclaimer about the name of this chapter. You shouldn't take it too literally.

Yes, it's true that I named the chapter. Yes, it's true that we're going to discuss the five things you need to be successful within it. But I don't want you to skip back here to this part, take out your highlighter, and think that the job will be done after you read through these pages. I don't want you to ignore everything that we've talked about in the book up to this point. Because really, and I'm sure you've noticed, it all flows together—it's all of a piece with the previous part, and each chapter contains actions that you need to take to ensure the success of your own job, your HR function's work, or your organization, depending upon where you sit at the table.

So as we go over these five things, I want you to avoid looking at them as magic wands. I want you to instead think about how they interact with the domains that we've gone over in the preceding chapters, and particularly how they interact with the concept of *alignment*, the importance of which cannot be overstated. I want you to really think about how these five things apply to you, and how you can apply these five things to your business today, regardless of your role. As we near the close of the book and our time together, I want to call your attention to these five areas that are often missed by organizations when trying to find their way on the path to success.

Now, without any further ado, let's get to it. **The five things you need to be successful are:**

✓ Your lens
✓ Change enablement/marketing
✓ Never stop learning
✓ Perpetual beta
✓ Dream

Your Lens

I've spoken about the **lens** before. Being able to look at problems and devise solutions through the appropriate lens is a key trait in being able to be successful at *anything* you do, but I find that this specifically applies to the HR space, particularly as HR professionals try to reimagine and rethink what they're doing. When engaging in this reimagining, it's so very important to think about it through the lens of your audience rather than your own lens. As a person who is trying to deliver information and processes, get work done, and help employees be better at their jobs, you want to make sure that the information you're offering can actually be understood and used by your audience. And each audience speaks its own language (sometimes figuratively, but sometimes literally, particularly as a global workforce is more commonplace).

Let's look at things through the lens of an employee, for example. As an employee of an organization, when I interact with my HR contacts, I want (and need) to be able to get things done quickly, without a lot of pain, hassle, and pomp and circumstance. When I need to change my address, enroll in a new benefit, tell someone I'm taking a day off, check on my vacation balance, whatever the need might be, I'd like it to be simple. Easy, right? No, HR sucks at simple.

Steve Jobs, whose philosophy and products served as icons of complex simplicity, once famously said that "Simple is the hardest thing to do." Oftentimes, what we think of as a simple process is anything but. And as an HR professional or someone who is interested in changing the space, it's crucial that you understand that this simplicity of process must be applied through the appropriate lens, or it won't be simple at all. It might as well be in a different language if it's not thought through properly, using the lens of the intended audience.

One of the easiest transactions to call to mind when thinking about this sort of challenge is the change of address. This is probably one of the most common interactions that an employee will have with HR, and definitely one of the most reoccurring. In any kind of profession, you'll have your own jargon, your own language. HR has this in droves: FTE, comp-ratio, regrettable termination, SPD, LMS (as we spoke about in the previous chapter). Functions notoriously have their own language (and several dialects, at that).

Many HR managers will pat themselves on the back for electronic self-service (and again, I would encourage you not to use that word—direct access sits much better with the troops, and with good reason) portals where employees can enter their own updates to personal information. But there are still problems with these portals. For instance, most often, the first field an employee will see when asked about their new address is the "effective date." For an employee who doesn't necessarily speak the language of HR, this might not mean anything. An employee in one of my usability studies put it best when he joked: "To me, an effective date is getting a kiss at the end of the first date."

Jokes aside, the concept of speaking a language that people understand, through the lens that they look through, is absolutely a key concept. But it's not just employees with their own lens and language. Managers also have their own lens. Managers want to be able to get information and see information in a way that's specific to them—information that's about *their* workforce. They are paid to worry about *their* workforce, not another department's workforce, not another section of the industry's workforce, but *their* workforce. Nor are they paid to worry about information about their workforce that doesn't apply to the searches they're running. So one of the important factors of looking through the appropriate lens is personalization—being able to personalize how people obtain, consume, and interact with information based on their particular lens and the language they speak. An example of doing this successfully would be sending out information on performance reviews of salaried employees to the managers of salaried employees, rather than the managers of hourly employees.

Continuing to move up the chain, executives obviously have their own specific lens. I can tell you that no matter which organization you're dealing with, executives want information to be presented in a way that's visually appealing and prescriptive. They are exceptionally busy, exceptionally taxed individuals who don't want to read through piles of reports and try to pick out things that are important to them. They have other ways to spend their time. They want to be able to find things easily, and see things presented in ways that make sense at a glance. An executive is given information all day long and is asked to constantly make on-the-spot decisions about that information—and those decisions likely aren't about trivial things, either. So knowing that an executive needs to be spoken to in this particular language and through this particular lens can greatly enhance the communication, alignment, and agility within an organization's chain of command.

But what about those who fall outside the chain of command? What about the all-important recruitment and engagement efforts that stretch beyond current employees into potential hires as well? Applicants definitely have their own lens and their own language. Their lens is one of relative uncertainty; they're not sure if they want to work at your organization yet, but they might be willing to apply. Why risk turning them off with jargon and antiquated processes that don't impart a user-friendly experience? Chances are, if your application process is off-putting, they're not going to finish it. But if they do, it's going to be in the back of their mind as a potential red flag when it comes to deciding whether or not to accept your offer.

If HR can see past its own lens and start shifting its mind-set to truly empathize with the viewpoints of other players, success can be well within reach.

Change Enablement/Marketing

The second thing you must understand and incorporate in order to be successful is **change enablement (or change management/ marketing).** The terms go hand in hand for the purposes of this discussion, although change enablement is really the next generation of change enablement—that mind-set shift, that "thinking differently," can lead to radical and wonderful things in organizations, industries, and society at large.

Typically when we talk about change enablement, we are talking about training. In the old-school days of HR, rolling out new processes and technology meant spending a lot of time and money on training. HR would offer classes on how to use email, Microsoft Excel, PowerPoint, an organization's particular network, and on it goes. Because of the expense and sluggish deployment of these technologies in the past, it wasn't possible for many employees to use all of the systems, nor was it possible to train many employees at a time on those systems. But as we've talked about at length, the shifting landscape of technology, which is now more instantaneous and user-friendly, has enabled companies to make greater use of cheaper tools, and incorporate those tools faster. Now, instead of 1 percent of your employees using a technology, 99 percent of the employees are using the technology. Your focus must be different now, and broader in scope—you have more people in more departments to deal with. And to succeed, you have to manage the 99 percent, not the 1 percent.

> To succeed, you have to manage the 99 percent of your employees, not the 1 percent.

This widening of the scope of technology use (and ownership) means that change enablement/change management today has taken on more of a communication/marketing flavor than the training flavor of the past. When I say communication/marketing, I mean all the internal persuasion and branding that goes into convincing employees that this change is a good thing, that there's something *in it for them* (the What's In It For Me factor we were talking about earlier). The workforce needs to understand how it's helpful to them, and how it's helpful to the organization—and all of this needs to be communicated in such a way that it makes the employee engage with the organization's mission and align with it organically, rather than feeling as though they are being asked to lock into something that's useless to everyone except the top brass.

Now that the technologies that we're using in the workplace are taking on some of that SaaS-oriented usability we talked about earlier, we might need to worry less about training and more about usefulness. Thinking about the way that we use technology as consumers for a moment—we all use Facebook, and we all use LinkedIn. Did we go to a class to get trained on those applications? NO! These tools are out there and they are designed to be consumed in a way that allows for instant access and intuitive use. And we use them because they are useful to us; there's a strong value proposition, whether it's socialization or networking or professional gain or self-promotion (all for free, no less). So to get employees to use a tool or process, there has to be a strong incentive surrounding the What's In It For Me equation.

In many organizations, for example, employees don't take time to fill out their talent profile. If you're not familiar with a talent profile, it's essentially an employee's baseball card. Using these talent profiles, I, as a business leader, can make decisions about how and where to use employees, how to staff employees, how to think about the futures and careers of those employees, and how to recruit and hire into the future based on whom and what I'm going to need. It's incredibly useful for a leadership position; however, for whatever reason, many employees probably don't log into the system to fill out their talent profile. Yet, when it comes to their own personal talent profile—and here I mean LinkedIn or Facebook—they're on it in a flash.

So the question I have to ask myself, then, is why? Why won't my employees do something for me that they'll do for themselves on their own time (and groom/update it constantly, on top of that)? The answer is simple: They don't see the value in it. Maybe the employees of an organization noticed that every time a job above theirs opened up, the company would advertise it to the outside world first, rather than look internally to promote one of its own. So why bother filling it out? They have a good point there, and if we had looked at it from their lens, we would have seen that.

The same thing can be said for social-type applications that are meant to foster collaboration in the workplace around group projects. A company will roll out a new collaborative technology only to hear the sound of crickets, and no other fanfare. And yet, all around them, the managers can see employees talking, texting, emailing, and making phone calls—but not using the collaborative tool that the company has spent time and money rolling out. But what's in it for these employees? Are the executives collaborating? Is the office one that has a culture of collaboration? Is data taken from the collaboration and turned into actionable insight and prescriptive measures? Is the notion of collaboration—and the tool itself—aligned with the efforts of the business as a whole?

These aren't questions that your employees are going to come into your office and ask, by the way. All you're going to hear are those crickets. These are questions that you're going to have to anticipate and answer with your internal marketing and communication departments, making it clear to your employees that there is value in it for them and that you're committed to showing them that value. You have to get people excited, and you have to spark their passions. You have to make them *want* to participate; it can't just be another ho-hum memo coming down from on high asking them to do something that doesn't feel useful to them.

I often liken it to a movie premiere—there's a timeline of trailers and teasers starting about ten weeks out with a little information, and then an ad campaign with on-set sneak peeks, and then action figures, and then advance reviews, and then an increase in advertising volume, on and on up until the planned premiere of the movie. By opening night, the studio has built up such excitement and consumer drive to see the movie that opening night is looked at by many theatergoers as a chance to take part in this *experience* that they've been hearing so much about. But what if the big opening fails? The next thing you know, the movie's on Netflix, or iTunes, or heaven forbid, DVD. If the movie tanks on opening night, it's going to be a failure for the rest of its existence. The same can be said of many of these processes and tools that are rolled out—we expect a lot, and if the tool doesn't meet our expectations or it isn't rolled out with enough excitement to get people engaged, it's very hard to ever get people to adopt that process or technology.

Ultimately, any mind-set shift requires two phases: The shift itself, and the drive to get others to understand and buy into that shift. If you make both happen, success is sure to follow.

Never Stop Learning

In life as in the workplace, change is the only constant. It seems as though the pace of change is picking up exponentially, too, as we have more advanced and widespread technology at our disposal. And it's not going backward anytime soon—we can only move forward. Companies of all shapes and sizes have to make a conscious commitment to keep up with this change, to move forward with the times, or be forever left behind. It's sink or swim.

I'm fortunate in my career that my days are spent constantly plugging in to different outlets in this universe of flux. I get to connect with innovators firsthand, learning about successful strategy across many different industries. Despite the mornings where it takes me a couple minutes to figure out where in the world I am, it's absolutely worth it, mostly because I'm someone who is driven by a hunger to keep learning and growing, to keep moving with the currents of change.

But there's a very good reason that I see myself as fortunate, and that's because not everyone gets the opportunity to be constantly thrust into the crucible of one's industry and allowed to percolate with diverse and brilliant leaders. Your average executive, manager, or employee must carve out these opportunities for himself or herself, putting in the time and effort to engage and educate in a lifelong way.

In the past, just as we thought of learning to mean the dry training modules that HR would have to roll out alongside new IT processes, we might have thought that learning took some typical forms, like talking to a friend or coworker or attending a conference. But today, like everything else, the landscape of learning has changed. Now, in a world where more information is available to be consumed than ever before, learning means putting yourself out there, being willing to watch and learn from other companies—even your competitors. Chances are good that they want to learn from you as much as you want to learn from them, and they're willing to share. Obviously this doesn't extend to the secret formula for Coca-Cola, or the proprietary design secrets of Apple, but to general strategy, information, and best practices—all of these are out there for the taking, ready to be studied and emulated.

All companies and people want to learn, and all companies and people want to get better, but many are afraid to ask. Don't be afraid. Get involved in group networking—local chapters of professional association meetings, for example. In addition to the usual in-person outlets, the Internet is obviously the place to be when it comes to networking, information exchange, and the generation of big and bold ideas. Using resources like Twitter—which unfairly gets a bad rap as the place to be if you want to hear what strangers are eating for breakfast—is a wonderful way to keep learning. If you follow me on Twitter @jasonaverbook, you'll be pleasantly surprised to find that I'm *not* talking about what I'm having for breakfast (who has time to eat breakfast?!), and you'll see that I'm able to interact with leaders and news sources, curate my Twitter feed to collect the best articles and resources out there in real-time, and build my network—and my idea bank. Social networking tools provide a fantastic way to learn and share, and you should be a part of that. We need your voice and your ideas, too (and sometimes even your breakfast food)!

Resources internal to your company are essential, too. In the spirit of alignment and breaking out of those silos and stovepipes, you should look around at your fellow executives, managers, or employees and see what everyone else is up to. Create a culture of openness, of collaboration. Really work at sharing ideas and keeping a record of them—and use that brainstorming and energy later on.

I worked with a client who started a "Champions" group at his organization—it was about 150 people strong, and made up of people who volunteered or who were solicited because of their reputation for being both thoughtful and outspoken on their views in the organization. The group acted like a focus group within the company, always responding to and generating new ideas. To **never stop learning** also means to never stop listening, and to understand that oftentimes the best ideas can come from people and places that you wouldn't expect them to. People like those in this group are likely to drive change, because they come at a problem from a different lens. If you want to continue to journey forward rather than stand still, you'll need these people in your lives—stop, listen, and learn from them. Then return the favor.

Perpetual Beta

Perpetual Beta is a popular term that's cropping up more often; it's basically a tech-savvy way of saying, "You're never done." It's also a monumental shift for people, particularly those who work in less agile, more established organizations where a product isn't rolled out until every last bug has been tweaked, every last knob and nut and bolt spit-shined to perfection. In today's economy, with its nimble products and often-esoteric assets (a widget isn't just a physical widget anymore), things tend to move faster and change on the fly. And we're forgiving of that change, and can even invite it.

Over the decades, we've been used to going through a process for a product launch: Working on it in secret, having a go-live party, rolling the technology out into the world, and then moving on to the next thing. But in the world we live in today, we can never stop continuing to advance what we're doing—we can't start a website or blog and then leave it to collect dust. We can't actually put out a piece of new technology and never check again to see if it's been used or not. We don't send our kids to school and never check up on how they're doing, go to parent-teacher conferences, or ask to see report cards. That's just not how it works. Instead, we live in a world of perpetual beta—where we're constantly exploring, constantly gathering feedback, and constantly trying new things. Hopefully, this process will help us continue to improve, making it worth the risk and bumps along the way.

But going back to shifting and adjusting your lens, perpetual beta requires looking at things differently. Engineers and employees (not only them, but just as two examples) are used to projects that have beginning and end dates. In today's world, those things blur. Things can be updated, shapes can be changed, and so to compete, *your* products and things must be continually updated and changed.

Even hard-copy assets, such as books, have to be updated—with up-dated editions, added prefaces, and interactive components. This way, those assets live on, and they stay relevant. People continue to engage with the asset, learn from it, and talk about it.

So this is all to say that the world can't be viewed as a one-and-done kind of place anymore. In the world of business technology, in particular, once you go live, that's actually the start of your journey. For HR, that means that once you've rolled out a process, you then have to do the work of analyzing that process, tweaking it, making it better, and seeing what you can get out of it. What kind of information are you getting out of the process? How can you take that information and make prescriptive analyses for people? And once that happens, how does that effect change in an organization? Perpetual beta means being willing to shift, to change, and to continue to innovate using the tools at hand to glean different types of information, or to use those tools differently to drive different outcomes.

Gone are the days of putting people on a project and telling them when they can expect to be moved on to the next thing. Now, if an organization wants to be successful, it has to achieve (and impart) the perpetual beta mind-set to its workforce—getting them used to staying on a project, trying new things, and being at peace with the fact that some things are going to fail and that there's still value in that.

Dream

Of the many resources I've sought out that have ended up changing *my* life and lens, one of my favorites is the book *The Radical Leap* by Steve Farber. Leap, in addition to being a fantasti-cally apt verb, is an acronym: Farber uses it to stand for Love, Energy, Audacity, and Proof. The premise behind his book is that in order to do anything in today's world, you have to *love* what you're doing. If you love what you're doing, you're going to gain the *energy* to do something *audacious*. And in order to keep that energy contained in a positive cycle, you'll have to have *proof*, for yourself and others, that the audacious thing gave something back to your life. I think that's a beautiful notion, and it's absolutely inspired this final secret for success, which is to always, always, always **dream.**

My job is not a part-time job. I love it, but it's all-consuming. I can't just do it and go home at the end of the day—it's all the time, anytime, anyplace. In order to sustain that kind of pace, I've really got to love what I do. In order to reimagine work, reimagine business, and reimagine how our world works—and to have the energy and passion to impart that to my clients—I have to truly wear that love on my sleeve, giving my clients the energy to do audacious things and prove to other people that those things work. If I don't do that, and I don't continue to dream, it's very easy to get bogged down. I'll stop growing. I'll stop succeeding. And so will my clients. Without dreams, I'll succumb to inertia.

Inertia is an insidious, powerful thing. I was recently at a software conference where I really got a sense of just how powerful inertia can be. A vendor that I was speaking to told me that of all his competitors, the biggest competition for his software was "no decision." He said that 30 percent of the time that he competes with other software companies for a client, his software wins the day. Five percent of the time, he loses to a competitor. But an overwhelming 65 percent of the time, he loses to "no decision." "No decision" most certainly translates to inertia on the end of the client. It's likely the client stopped dreaming of a different solution, a better way.

We live in an era where the easiest answer is "don't change," even as the world around us is changing so rapidly. Restrictions on money, time, and energy sap us of the will to love what we do, to have the passion to push things through. And these kinds of conflicting messages will continue to drag us down if we succumb to them. We know the world is changing, that business is changing, our employees are changing, and the workforce itself is changing. But we also hear the damning chorus of voices telling us that change will be too hard, and that "no decision" is the best decision.

I recently had dinner with a friend who was telling me that in order to get someone hired in his organization, once the higher-ups have made the decision to hire that person, that person's resume and application had to go to fourteen different people to have that information entered into the system before the file is marked as "HIRED" and the employee can start working. I asked him the obvious question: "WHY?! Why does it take three weeks for a new hire to start? Why does it have to go through fourteen people?"

His response almost made me fall out of my chair. "It's the way we've always done it."

Of course, I wanted to know why he didn't change it. And of course, he told me it was too hard to change, that there would be too much internal pushback. And that, my friends, is the kind of thinking that kills us—the kind of inertia that will suck us down into the muck instead of helping us soar to the sky.

My most-repeated advice on the issue of how to succeed is to get out of this mind-set that making no decision—or no change—is an acceptable decision. You *must* try in order to succeed. You must sometimes have failures in order to keep trying. You must try in order to learn. And if you're not trying, if you're not changing, you're never going to move forward.

Success isn't moving backward, and it's certainly not standing still. It's that-a-way.

Chapter Ten

A Community Call to Action

SO here we are, at the end of our journey together.

Scratch that. That's not true at all. I'd prefer to think of it as the beginning—the place where all of our preparation will help us get the running start we'll need to take a stunning leap from the now into the next. We live in an unprecedented time: One where the only constant is change, and one where that change constantly gives us the opportunity to excel in ways we never thought possible.

But we can only do that if we embrace the change; if we reach out of our silos and across the aisles to better understand what our organizational neighbors are up to. If we are not in HR, embracing that change means working to achieve alignment and articulation of vision so that HR can pursue, hire, and retain talent that fits with that vision. If we are in the IT space, embracing that change means seeking solutions that promote agility, smooth out processes, and create a more nimble workforce. If we are in the HR space, embracing that change means truly understanding what our responsibilities are—and how those responsibilities differ from what they might have been in the past. We all have a stake in the future, and the only way to get there is together. Together, we all make up a community dependent on this change, and I want this book to have served as a rallying call to all of you to act—both on your own and together.

The eight domains discussed in this book can serve as your map, a guide to what that action might look like. There's not one way to go about achieving these goals; each organization has its own people, its own assets, its own metrics, and its own strengths. Your methods should play to those strengths, always keeping the larger corporate vision in mind. Remember these eight domains as you move forward, manifesting the more aligned, agile tomorrow you most wish to inhabit:

✓ **Reimagine HR.** HR can no longer say, "This is the way we've always done it, so this is the way we'll always do it." That excuse is no longer valid. In order to move forward efficiently, HR needs to take advantage of the amazing tools made available by the changing times. Part of becoming fluent in these tools means reimagining the scope of what it means to be an HR professional.

✓ **Create agility.** Change is a funny thing. It will trample you if you're not looking, but if you can harness it, it can take you on one heck of a ride. Don't get trampled. Instead, stay in front of change. Read. Meet other people. Use social technologies to gather information from experts near and far. Advocate change and be the agent for that change.

✓ **Identify talent.** If LinkedIn knows more about your greatest assets (your people) than you do, then you're in trouble. Work to identify talent within your own organization (and use tools like LinkedIn to your advantage, grooming and identifying the talent from without as well) and learn how to play to the strengths of that talent, properly retaining, developing, and incenting them. Don't let your talent management strategy begin and end with recruitment.

✓ **Increase engagement.** Like the other domains, this one overlaps with the one before it. When we talk about increasing engagement, we're talking about making that investment in our ultimate asset: Our talent pool. This is especially important today, as the generational composition of the workforce is shifting. Along with that shift in age comes a shift in values and philosophy, and we need to be responsive to that. Understand that increasing engagement should be a constant process and not an intermittent one; engagement should be promoted and measured in real-time using real-time tools.

✓ **Foster collaboration.** Just as the business day is no longer confined to 9-to-5, an employee is no longer restricted by the cubicle walls. Changing technologies are making wonderful collaborative tools available to organizations of all sizes. Smaller organizations can now have the collaborative impact of a much larger workforce, and the larger organizations truly have an opportunity to change the conversation about innovation from the factory floor up. It's also not enough to pay lip service to collaboration—like engagement, it's a living, breathing, organic thing that can only thrive in a host that truly values it.

✓ **Think differently about measuring.** HR can no longer count heads. That's not good enough. We need to move to truly *making heads count.* How do we do this? By employing strategic initiatives to collect data that really means something to an organization as opposed to just those who are reading the data with an HR lens. By taking these measurements within the context of a larger organization, and not just the HR silo. By making sure there's an accurate and easily accessible place where all of these measurements reside. By presenting the information to people who can do something with it in a way that's easily digestible and understandable.

✓ **Keep your head in the cloud.** With technology moving from the world of on-premise software to the cloud, and SaaS making it easier than ever before to deploy new technologies and keep those technologies updated, it doesn't make sense to tether yourself down with clunky solutions. It's much more cost-effective to subscribe versus buy and maintain nowadays. Not to mention your workforce will be more efficient: Every moment they spend waiting on an upgrade is a moment they could be generating revenue. What if they could have instant access instead? Time is money, and both add up quickly.

✓ **Take ownership over technology.** We're all technologists now. It's not good enough to just wash your hands of IT, or blame IT for the problems you as an HR person are experiencing. The two departments must work together, now more than ever before, particularly in this age of SaaS and instant access. But more than that, HR has to take ownership of the process and technology it wants to use, doing more than handing IT a punch list. By thinking strategically about what features and tools it needs, HR will be able to work together with IT to outfit the organization with processes and technology that will help ensure success.

· · · ·

So there you have it, there's the map.

Just keep going. Keep pushing. Keep dreaming. We will get there. Where you ask? We will get from Now to Next.

Another infusion of knowledge...

CPSIA information can be obtained at www.ICGtesting.com
Printed in the USA
BVOW11*1108210814

362837BV00001B/1/P

9 781939 758361